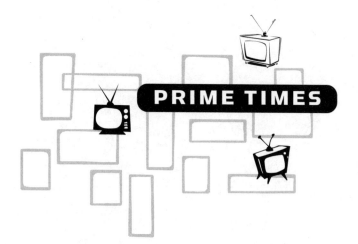

PRIME TIMES

Prime Times

Writers on Their Favorite TV Shows

EDITED AND WITH AN INTRODUCTION BY
DOUGLAS BAUER

CROWN PUBLISHERS
NEW YORK

791.4575
Pri

Grateful acknowledgment is made to the following for permission to reprint previously published material:

"Amos 'n' Andy and Civil Rights on TV," from *Colored People,* by Henry Louis Gates Jr., copyright © 1994 by Henry Louis Gates Jr. Used by permission of Alfred A. Knopf, a division of Random House, Inc.

"The Mary Tyler Moore Show," by Nora Ephron, reprinted by permission of International Creative Management, Inc. Copyright © 1977 by Nora Ephron. First appeared in *Esquire.*

Published by Crown Publishers, New York, New York.
Member of the Crown Publishing Group, a division of Random House, Inc.
www.crownpublishing.com

Published simultaneously in paperback by Three Rivers Press, a division of Random House, Inc.

CROWN is a trademark and the Crown colophon is a registered trademark of Random House, Inc.

Printed in the United States of America

Design by Lauren Dong

Library of Congress Cataloging-in-Publication Data
Prime times: writers on their favorite television shows / edited and with an introduction by Douglas Bauer.—1st ed.
1. Television programs—United States. I. Bauer, Douglas.
PN1992.3.U5P75 2004
791.45'75—dc22   2003019805

ISBN 1-4000-4754-4

10 9 8 7 6 5 4 3 2 1

First Hardcover Edition

CONTENTS

INTRODUCTION

I have a friend, a painter and a very fine one. Some years ago, he agreed to join a few fellow artists who were renting a New England farmhouse for part of the summer. The plan, besides escaping the city heat, was to spend their days capturing on canvas the pastoral surroundings, the hills and dense green woods, the sloping pastures, barn-dotted. I should say that my friend is a deeply urban creature, born and raised in Queens, someone whose need for both high and popular culture is akin to his need for oxygen. So he hesitated before accepting the invitation, and it was well into the group's first day of work when one of his housemates left her easel and walked a distance through the field to where he'd set up his, in order to compare their versions of nature. Once she reached him, they nodded greetings and she stepped around to view his canvas and saw that he was painting a montage of television sets.

I love this story for what it says about my friend's stubborn sensibility, but I tell it here because it gives me the chance to say that from its birth, television has for good and ill been a deeply embedded feature of the landscape. I mean this in a larger sense, of course—not only do we see the cultural landscape on television, we see the influence of television everywhere in the landscape— but it's still a groaningly bad pun of a metaphor, I know. It just serves my purposes too perfectly to resist.

Since this perception of TV, as both a reflection of and a force that shapes the culture, is hardly original, I asked some of the finest writers of our time to make it so. I was sure that by inviting them to chronicle life's occasions through the prism of television, to tap some savored moments from their viewing and real lives, the result would be a rich collection of wise and witty and uniquely personal accounts.

Thanks wholly to their talents, that's precisely what this book is.

But I'd also had a hunch that it might be something much more: a kind of social mosaic of the past half century, the pieces, brought together, making a highly entertaining anthropology. And I'm delighted to say it's that as well—an eclectic gathering of autobiography, memory, and blade-sharp observation, all wonderfully bound by the common experience of watching lives on television while living one's own, and the intimate intermingling of the two when there's a particularly keen need for inspiration or escape, counsel or company.

People were free to write about the present or the past, an episode or a series, a single event or a broadcast discussion of societal behavior for which TV provides an apt vocabulary. A marvelous minority chose current shows, while one contributor, Mark Leyner, took the opportunity to wildly invent (a zany riff on the story behind the story of *Hawaii Five-0*), but most of these pieces are exquisite recollections. Here, the particular programs act as televisual madeleines, whole vivid universes of the writers' pasts returned on the memory of what they loved to watch. This was not all that surprising, once I thought about it, since the invitation implies a strong devotion to a show or, if not that, the singular impact of someone or something extraordinary appearing on a television screen. And devotions of such depth, impacts of such resonance, are finally visceral and tend to occur when we are young and our minds are originally malleable—when, as April Bernard says in writing about the Patrick McGoohan series *Secret Agent*, "Irony . . . was lost on me," which meant that, as a young girl, she "took *Secret Agent* straight, and I took it quietly, with awe."

Alan Lightman, whose "best television memories," like Bernard's, like those of many others, also "come from that long-ago period of my childhood," was equally mesmerized by *The Twilight Zone*, every episode of which "was true." Some twenty-five years later, Virginia Heffernan and her little brother watched *Davey and Goliath*, a Sunday-morning theology-lite cartoon show, oblivious to the TV room catching fire around them. Mesmerized indeed.

Many of the recollections, written from the perspective of *some* point before adulthood, invoke the very day the first set arrived and was reverently switched on—the screen stirring lazily to life, yielding its images in the way of early Polaroid snapshots slowly cohering—and there was the sensation of a " 'We've got liftoff' moment," as Sven Birkerts remembers in his rumination on the pioneering world of black and white. Several others exactly call up the finer physical details of the set itself and what spot in the house it occupied. In Henry Louis Gates Jr.'s house, "[it] was located in the living room, where it functioned like a fireplace in the proverbial New England winter. I'd sit in the water in the galvanized tub in the middle of our kitchen, watching the TV [including *Amos 'n' Andy*] in the next room." Susan Cheever's whole family watched *Father Knows Best* on an Emerson, "a small rectangular black box crowned with long, adjustable antennae resting on a wrought-iron cocktail table near the sofa." "As with most of the television that matters," Michael Gorra observes, "[the] viewing is in memory inseparable from the company and the time and the place," and in *his* memory it's Sunday night at nine o'clock, time for *Masterpiece Theatre* on PBS, the TV perched "on the wide raised hearth of a fireplace we almost never used."

Like Gorra, some contributors, while also looking back, summon a somewhat later time, early adolescence to adulthood, when they and television shared episodes of that ultimate reality show entitled *life*. There's repeated testimony, in tones ranging from self-mocking wryness to tender affection to straight-out appreciation, paying thanks to TV or someone on it for being a kind of spiritual ally. David Shields, describing the first years of *Monday Night Football*, makes a strong case for Howard Cosell. (I know; just read it.) And Lan Samantha Chang felt a subliminal empathy for the feckless castaways of *Gilligan's Island*, who were, like her own family, stranded in a foreign place, her parents and grandmother having fled China and washed up on "a tiny island of Chinese memories and customs, surrounded by vast shimmering fields of alfalfa, corn, and soybeans," in Appleton, Wisconsin.

Richard Bausch, newly married and newly trying to write, happened accidentally on *The Dick Van Dyke Show* one morning and remembers: "The fact that [Van Dyke's character] Rob Petrie was a writer gave off a wonderful sense of the ordinariness of trying to make things up for a life's work. No, not the ordinariness— the honorableness." Nora Ephron, on the other hand, is grateful to Rob Petrie's wife, that is, to Mary Tyler Moore, though only some years later when she became Mary Richards and moved to Minneapolis and had her own show. "It meant a lot to me," Ephron writes, "the second time I was single and home alone on Saturday night to discover that Mary Tyler Moore was home, too."

Elizabeth McCracken and Stephen McCauley are also grateful. "There have," McCracken says, "been times in my life—I'm not kidding about this—when I have been wretchedly unhappy about something, and that's when I actually look at the TV listings to see if and when *America's Funniest Home Videos* is on. . . . It won't erase my problems, but it sure as hell won't remind me of them." As for McCauley, he's thankful not to a single character or show but to the "unabashed awfulness" of a whole category, the ineffable world of infomercials, for helping him through a bleak, bad patch of life. "Was it possible," he asks, "that what [I was] experiencing when [I] watched these half-hour dramas with their obsequious hucksters and their horrid staging . . . was honest-to-God catharsis?" I suspect Douglas Rushkoff might say, yes, it could have been, since he remembers, when watching *Lost in Space* or *Mystery Science Theater 3000*, the sympathetic comradeship of television at a time in *his* life when "it was just me and the tube against an otherwise nonsensical world."

Looking, also with real appreciation, to the nearly opposite pole of TV history, Lloyd Schwartz thinks, "It's just possible that my love of language—my *interest* in language—began with Gracie Allen." Acknowledging his debt to Gracie as a source of inspiration for his poetry, Schwartz argues that her seemingly ditzy declarations on *The Burns and Allen Show* were as tidy and efficiently allusive as haiku when you got down to parsing them.

Besides the many vernaculars of gratitude, you also hear a voice running through these accounts of what might be called, somewhat paradoxically, a sharply incisive nostalgia. Which is to say that while a fondness for a show is consistently sounded, everyone here speaks of TV's coincidental power to transport us, depending as it does on the time slot we, ourselves, happen to be occupying, what the lead-ins in our lives are, what's playing on the competing channels of place and work and love. Growing up in small-town North Carolina, Jill McCorkle embraced the whole globe of early sitcoms, but her affection for most of them was somewhat checked, stopped at the state line by the mystery of their distant locales—Manhattan and Queens and Chicago and Minneapolis. On the other hand, Mayberry, North Carolina, where Andy Taylor and Barney Fife and Aunt Bee and Opie lived, was, McCorkle writes, "my town"; to turn off an episode of *The Andy Griffith Show* would have been like "turning off a home movie." And in her tribute to the immortal Barbara Stanwyck, playing Victoria Barkley on *The Big Valley,* Jayne Anne Phillips recalls that even before the show ended, "the Tet Offensive was raging [and] I stopped watching much TV. . . . Maybe America couldn't watch Victoria Barkley with a straight face anymore: There was so little civility, sanity, and class in our country by 1969."

Or now, for that matter, Nick Hornby would argue, explaining his "undying love," as a Brit, for *The West Wing*. One of those few writing about a current program, Hornby shows we can be as nostalgic for what *isn't* as for what once was, pointing out that the people running our country on the show "are smart, ironic, and thoughtful; that's how we know that what we're watching is only a TV show. . . . If we wanted to listen to pedants and dullards, we'd tune in to C-SPAN, or our national equivalents." And James Alan McPherson finds a similarly welcome refuge, in what Hornby calls "the realms of fantasy," in the eternal verities of the original *Star Trek* series, which "dramatized how human beings . . . acting on feelings with which we all could identify, resolved conflict after conflict after conflict."

This sounds sort of like the premise for *Survivor,* except that *its* strategy for conflict resolution boils down to the Rule of Last One Standing. Which is fine with Phyllis Rose, who's just glad it isn't her. As she observes, "From *Your Show of Shows* to *Northern*

Exposure . . . television has gone to great pains to create on-screen communities of which one wants to be a part." Indeed, it's the sense of that very pull that sparked the idea for this anthology— the way we vicariously leave our living rooms for those of our favorite shows. But as far as Rose is concerned, the appeal of *Survivor* is quite the contrary; it's the luxury of watching, from the comfort of your home, those competing tribes of "people who make you want to run in the other direction."

Not so for Susan Perabo and her fast fidelity to the Hortons, "Tom and Alice and their five adult children," who've been weathering preposterous calamities, and inflicting more than a few of their own, for almost forty years on *Days of Our Lives*. Introduced to the show by her beloved grandmother, Perabo believes it's soap operas, not *Survivor* and all the Roman-spectacle lunacies it has spawned, that were the first and are the true reality shows. Why? Because "*Days of Our Lives*, like life, exhibits no definable arc of story, just an endless series of fits and starts."

It seems only right to end with the soaps, as vital today as they were at the creation, when screens were the size of a telescope lens and the naive thrill of watching felt, fittingly enough, like peering *through* one to watch civilizations on other planets. Planets that I, too—growing up in the middle of the country in the middle of the just-completed century—wanted desperately to visit. I was maybe nine or ten when we got a set. The dealer drove it in his pickup from his shop on the square of our tiny Iowa town, out to my family's farm. His name was Dick Charls and, as you can imagine, he occupied a special place in the village hierarchy as the person, the only person for miles, with the power to hook you up to the world. A sort of electronic herald.

I remember, one Saturday afternoon, tuning in to the Iowa– Ohio State football game, which would decide the Big Ten conference championship, something Iowa hadn't won in decades.

For me, at that age, sports was what there was in life and I sat inches from the screen, watching with a nearly tactile fervor.

This would not be unusual—a sports-crazed boy rooting for his team—except that I was not actually watching the *game*. No local station was carrying it, but some ingenious improviser back at the studio in Des Moines had come with an idea to train a camera on a flat graph of a football field, the ten-yard lines running vertically on the screen. It was a crude illustration at best, the kind of thing an uninspired third-grader would come up with in art class on a hot spring afternoon.

But here's the thing. Superimposed on this field was a football-shaped icon. In memory, it resembled some mutant oblong insect that had crawled inside the set and meandered out past the bulbous tubes and nest of wires to the front, behind the screen. I'm thinking now that it might have been a kind of magnet because, as the station played the radio broadcast of the game, someone unseen behind the flat-graphed field—using a paired magnet, I'm guessing—moved the icon left and right, most unsteadily, to represent the action of each play.

That was it; the sum and substance of what there was to watch. And I was riveted, shouting and cursing, alternately suffering and giddy with elation as the little football wobbled in one direction, then the other, and I see vividly still its final movement, a weaving, drunken slide to the bottom of the screen, as though the insect repellent had finally kicked in—the desperate scramble of the Ohio State quarterback being chased and tackled to end the game.

Obviously I could have simply listened on the radio and "seen" as much of what was happening, which is to say nothing. But I needed to experience such a significant event in a way that gave me more than radio's merely aural moment. I sought this new phenomenon—movement on a screen in my living room. Even if that movement were nothing more than a cockroach-football inching back and forth, a cinematic display one very small step up from the stations' nightly test pattern. Which, Barry Hannah writes in his remembrance of early TV comedians, he and his boyhood friends did sometimes watch, because, "Even still life on the tube promised another world."

I offer my memory simply as evidence that, like my friend painting landscapes of TV sets, like each of the gifted writers gathered here, I know how it is to want the world on television.

PART ONE

AT THE MOMENT

THE WEST WING

Nick Hornby

"I've got a friend who works in the White House," a friend told me when I professed my undying love for *The West Wing*. "And he says it's nothing like that at all." Well, duh. All I need now is for someone to point out that small dinosaurs were never used as telephone receivers, not even in Fred Flintstone's day, and my viewing pleasure will have been ruined forever. Here's just one of the ways that Jeb Bartlet's presidency differs from its real-life counterpart: No one who works for Bartlet would be dull-witted enough to make that observation in the first place. Bartlet's people are smart, ironic, and thoughtful; that's how we know that what we're watching is only a TV show, and that's why we watch it. If we wanted to listen to pedants and dullards, we'd tune in to C-SPAN, or our national equivalents. (Listen to any kind of parliamentary or congressional debate and one is struck by the *otherness* of politicians: They're like no one you've ever met, and no one you would wish to meet. How are these people supposed to represent us when they are not of our species? I'd happily meet up with Josh and Toby and Sam for a drink once a week, and that's something else that places *The West Wing* in the realms of fantasy.)

The West Wing contains no expletives, so they don't have to be deleted. Bartlet is faithful to his wife, and we have not seen him lie to his nation. He is well-read, and he can spell (although if you ask me, his surname could use an extra *t*). He is religious, but in a gentle, New Testament kind of way, and we have seen him eviscerate religious bigots. He has knowledge of, and an interest in, countries other than his own. He seems to have no desire to appease wealthy special-interest groups. He was elected fair and square, as far as we know. Oh, *The West Wing* is made up, all right.

And yet, of course, the series knows its onions. It has political hotshots like Peggy Noonan among its advisers, and it feels real, to this viewer at least; *The West Wing* is not fantastical in that sense. It doesn't play fast and loose with the political process, nor, at the time of writing, have we seen Jeb Bartlet in hand-to-hand combat with international terrorists, or seizing the controls of the presidential jet. And the humorless, hard, cynical committee men and women who block the march of progressive democracy at every turn have the whiff of authenticity about them, too; we know these people are out there, skulking in corridors all over the world, because if they weren't, the world would be a nicer and more tolerant place, right?

And that is what I love about *The West Wing:* It earns, through its brilliant attention to the details of realpolitik, the right to offer an alternative to political cynicism. In sport—in soccer, anyway—they talk about fighting for the room to play; in other words, it's not possible to express yourself on the field unless you do the hard physical labor, the running and marking and covering and tackling. That is precisely what *The West Wing* does. The series clearly has ambitions beyond a painstaking portrayal of the political process; it has a lot of stuff to say about idealism and compromise and ambition and America itself. It's smart enough to know, however, that its themes would come across as glib if they were not given their brilliantly realized context. Compare *The West Wing* to, say, the facile political satire *Wag the Dog*, which wants to be hip and cynical but is actually too lazy and too credulous to convey anything but its own superciliousness. *The West Wing* is liberal and hopeful and sweet-natured, but extraordinarily, it's not naive; it's way too knowing for that.

If you don't believe me, watch the nineteenth episode of the show, entitled "Let Bartlet Be Bartlet." (Indeed, those who don't like *The West Wing* might argue that this is the only episode you need to watch, so neatly does it exemplify the show's themes and modus operandi, and, finally, its flaws.) "Let Bartlet Be Bartlet" is about an administration bogged down in the political mud; forty-five of the show's fifty minutes are spent depicting, extremely well, a group of individuals with an enormous amount of intellectual energy and nowhere to put it.

A dim TV series or film would have shown Bartlet attempting (and failing or succeeding, depending on the amount of shamelessness the creators felt they could get away with) to Save the World, to make some huge, unlikely—and easily comprehensible—political gesture. But *The West Wing* isn't dim, and so it alights upon two much smaller and complicated issues to illustrate the administration's problems. Bartlet is floating the idea ("dangling [his] feet in the water," in his timid phrase, and the question of how and why he has become so politically cautious is one the episode attempts to address) of nominating his own choices to sit on the Federal Election Commission, in an attempt to reform electoral finance. Meanwhile, Sam is talking to military representatives about the law preventing gays from serving in the armed forces. Both initiatives are crushed (the show is very good at political baddies, most of whom do little more than articulate, admittedly with an irritating smugness, the logic of the status quo, but who nevertheless make you want to form your own revolutionary movement). A typical TV script would have been swamped by the information it was attempting to impart, but in this one, not only do the fractious arguments in committee rooms feel knotty and real, they have an effortlessly attained subtext. I don't know whether you have ever attempted to write a screenplay, but those page margins are wide, and a commercial TV hour is short; to sustain simultaneous arguments about electoral reform and gays in the military—informed, researched arguments—while making it clear that these arguments are actually about something else . . . well, you need to be pretty good at your job to pull that off.

Toward the end of the episode, Bartlet's chief of staff, Leo McGarry, confronts Bartlet about the way his administration seems to be pulling its punches, and at this point the show departs from political reality: Bartlet, suddenly energized, vows to do something about it. Leo writes down the title of the episode on a piece of paper (he probably saw the caption at the beginning of the show), the president remembers why he wanted to be the president in the first place, and it all ends happily and inspirationally and, yes, let's be honest, cornily, with his key staff, wreathed in smiles, reiterating their loyalty and desire to serve. In real life, of course, Bartlet would have looked at Leo's piece of paper, laughed like a drain, and declared war on some small, defenseless country somewhere.

But if the episode ends up soggier than one might have wished (and *The West Wing* is, after all, soapy in its structure and narrative manipulation), it still makes you yearn to believe in its sincerity and its optimism; very few serious television programs—very few serious cultural artifacts of any kind—offer any hope at all. It's the curse of contemporary naturalism that prevents anyone from making the slightest suggestion of redemption; the world is not a redemptive place, and to suggest otherwise seems to connote feeble-mindedness. You can find plenty of crappy films and TV shows that cheer, but *The West Wing* has class and ambition, so its depiction of principled people remaining principled is especially brave. Cynicism and nihilism may have the virtue of accuracy, but, boy, it makes you tired; sometimes we need our culture to give us the strength to get up in the morning, and if you spend too much time watching things that insist on spelling out the way things are and always will be, it saps the will to live.

The liberal agenda of the show is brave, too. Of course, it would probably be impossible to create a TV series based around a Republican administration and expect anyone—even Republican voters—to sympathize with any of the protagonists ("In this week's episode: The president cuts welfare support for Latino single mothers and explains why the Kyoto agreement will hurt some rich guys he used to go to school with"). Even so, from this distance, on the other side of the Atlantic, it seems heartening, and vaguely mystifying, that a show that is so unambiguous in its views on gay rights, gun control, the religious right, the environment, and multiculturalism should have attracted a huge prime-time audience on a network station.

And why, you may be asking, would anyone in England care about a made-up American president? Your lot wouldn't care very much about a fictional prime minister. Well, we're used to things working only one way; when my first book, *Fever Pitch*, a memoir about being a soccer fan, was published in the United States, one reviewer quoted an admittedly arcane passage to demonstrate the problems an American readership was likely to encounter; meanwhile, we had sat through *Bull Durham* and *Eight Men Out* and *Field of Dreams*, failed to understand one line of dialogue in any of the three, and gamely professed to enjoy them anyway. We have long been used to the idea that we're always going to make more of an effort than you are. (And my American friend Sarah bought me a copy of the American Constitution, which now sits right by the TV, ready and eager for *West Wing* duty at any moment. As a consequence, I have even recently found myself envying you— your Constitution, that is. We have no equivalent, and it seems to me that an attempt to write one now would result in a much-needed national debate about who we are and what we want.)

But in any case, our attitude to American TV has changed. Throughout my childhood and young adulthood, we were the classy ones, and you were the purveyors of enjoyable fluff—which meant, inevitably, that we watched as much of your stuff as we could tune in to. Our Sunday afternoon children's TV hour, for example (we were only ever allowed an hour by the BBC), was frequently given over to a Dickens or Walter Scott adaptation, which wasn't even as much fun as it sounds. No surprise, then, that we lapped up *I Dream of Jeannie* and *Bewitched.* True, we were confused by rumors that in the States these were evening shows, aimed at adults; we were puzzled, too, by the apparently random laughter that appeared on the sound track, as if something funny was happening just out of earshot. But we all got the hang of American TV: It was something you watched instead of *Ivanhoe,* and it was always welcome in our house.

Meanwhile, British TV was at its artistic zenith. Gifted playwrights like Alan Bennett and Dennis Potter were given hours and hours of peak time to fill in whichever way they chose (Bennett's work was usually directed by Stephen Frears); Peter Cook, Dudley Moore, and the nascent Monty Python team were doing things that had never been done before. And then there was the costume-drama thing: Millions of us watched ambitious and successful adaptations of *War and Peace* and *The Forsyte Saga.* So brilliant was our output at the time, so intelligent and classy and innovative, that we gave ourselves permission to patronize American TV for the next three or four decades.

We began, grudgingly, to concede that you did the odd genre pretty well. Your cop shows (*Kojak, Starsky and Hutch*) were slicker and more glamorous than ours, but they were, you know, just cop shows. And when *Dallas* and *Dynasty* came along, we admired your sense of camp and your marvelous American vulgarity. But then it all started to get a little more serious; it was clear that American TV was beginning to get ideas above its station. With the advent of *Hill Street Blues,* we had to admit that your cop shows were not only slicker, but better-written and more innovative than ours. *Cheers,* and then *The Simpsons,* and, later, *Seinfeld* and *The Larry Sanders Show* hit our screens just at the time when it was clear we had forgotten how to make comedy. The enormous American internal market, which pays for enormous teams of talented writers, had finally asserted itself; a typical British comedy is written in its entirety and in perpetuity by one middle-aged (and frequently suburban) man, and is thus creaking like the Little House on the Prairie in a gale halfway through its first episode.

The significance of *The West Wing* and, now, *Six Feet Under* is that we cannot pretend they are generic: They are intelligent mainstream drama series, the sort of thing at which the BBC is supposed to excel. The success of these shows, and their obvious excellence, has prompted long, introspective, where-did-we-go-wrong articles in newspapers and magazines. "It is very rare for British television these days to hand its actors in a year lines as good as Bartlet, Toby, and Josh get weekly in *The West Wing,*" observed respected British journalist Andrew Billen in the posh current-affairs magazine *Prospect.* "It was not always so." The general feeling in Britain now is that your flagship shows are better than our flagship shows, and your rubbish beats our rubbish hands down; to older critics and commentators, those who can remember the BBC in its pomp, it's as if you've just given us a pasting at cricket.

It's not just the technical excellence of the show, the great writing (has a drama series ever gotten away with the sheer volume of words that *The West Wing* spews out week after week?), the terrific ensemble cast, and the production values. We, too, those of us who voted for this Labour government, have an alternative reality that we like to imagine sometimes. In this fantasy, an uxorious liberal with New Testament values and some mild but unmistakable Socialist tendencies marches in to 10 Downing Street and reinvigorates a country that has been stultifying for a couple of decades. He has energy and conviction, and he's not scared of upsetting the right; he doesn't waste his time on focus groups and spin doctors, and his main motivation is not reelection but the desire for change. In miserable reality, our prime minister is halfway through his second term of office and there's every prospect of a third, given the laughably shambolic state of the opposition: We have already let Blair be Blair, and there's nothing there. *The West Wing* is just as much a reminder to us of what we haven't got as it is to you.

We are, apparently, soon to be given the chance of watching our own version of *The West Wing*. My suspicion is that at best it will be smart, sharply written . . . and horribly realistic, in a way that would have been granted the approval of my friend's friend, the guy who works in the White House. We can do realism. Its characters will be cynical and compromised and opportunistic, in the way that real politicians are; and it won't do me any good at all. I don't need to know that politicians are all shits—I need to be enabled to imagine something different. That's what the best art is supposed to do, isn't it?

AMERICA, AMERICA, THIS IS YOU

Elizabeth McCracken

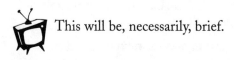 This will be, necessarily, brief.

1. IT'S FUNNY.

The golf balls that fly straight at the camera, the tiny dogs who jump into trees, the lady who gets stuck in her dishwasher, the giant dogs who are menaced by birds, the children who fall asleep in their suppers, the elderly dancers of the Alley Cat who fall over due to the domino effect and too much wedding champagne, the cranky children in school plays who take swings at each other . . . This is not an apologia. This is not a semiotic dissection. This is not an essay that asks, Are not the comedies of William Shakespeare simply Elizabethan England's Funniest Home Videos? There will be no comparison of *America's Funniest Home Videos* to poetry, fiction, any of the plastic arts, any of the performing arts, historical events, ancient myths, the works of Sigmund Freud, the

works of Carl Jung, the works of anyone with perhaps the exception of Allen Funt. (For the record: It's better than the works of
Allen Funt, to whom it is obviously in debt.) There will be no
wondering whether the unexamined and unvideotaped life is
worth living, or whether an inveterate videotapist has a life or
merely records the lives of others. There will be no discussion of
how we, as a people, need in these troubled times simple pleasures, especially ones that pull us together as a nation: our
heartaches, our blows to the groin, our weddings, our Columbus
Day pageants gone wrong, our golden retrievers who befriend
small, truculent kittens in our backyards. There will be no discussion of irony, allegory, symbolism, camp, or kitsch. There will be
no musing over whether Vin Di Bona (the show's executive producer) is celebrating America, or revealing America's shallowness
and love of water skiing. There will be no graphs analyzing which
piece of sporting equipment (golf ball, baseball, football, golf club,
soccer ball, goal post) produces the biggest laugh when accidentally applied to the human groin, and for how long, nor whether
the body-fat percentage of the recipient of the piece of sporting
equipment makes a difference.

ㅁ ㅁ ㅁ

This is a dirty secret, and if I had any sense, I would seek help for
it, not publication:

2. I HATED *SEINFELD*.

Maybe I hated it because when it was on so many people asked
me if I liked it. It was one of *those* shows—you know the kind: "I
hate TV but I really like . . ." To me, this is like saying, "I hate tod-
dlers but I really like two-year-olds." It's a TV show! And you like
it! Relax! The same people would sneer at someone who said, "I

don't like books but I really like Günter Grass," and with good reason.

There were a few things I hated about *Seinfeld.*

A. Everyone was always yelling.

B. The general premise—of it and plenty of other situation comedies of the past ten years—had to do with humiliation. Aha, you might say, brave words from a lover of *America's Funniest Home Videos,* and it's just like you to throw that in my face when I told it to you in the strictest confidence. But the fact is on *Seinfeld,* someone's pants falling down was the setup for an angst-filled twenty-two minutes about who saw the pants fall down, the ramification of the pants falling down, how to explain to other people that the pants didn't fall down on purpose, restagings of the pants falling down, denouement of the pants falling down. When did angst become so funny? By which I mean, when did it stop being really boring?

America's Funniest Home Videos is 100 percent angst-free. On *America's Funniest Home Videos,* as in life, pants falling down are a punchline, and even the guy who's lost the pants knows it.

Oh, you might say, pushing your luck; but that's *mean.* You're laughing *at* the guy who lost his pants, not *with* him.

This may be true. But I never could shake the feeling while watching *Seinfeld* that the actors were actually laughing *at me*, or would have, if they'd had the chance.

3. IT REQUIRES NOTHING OF ITS VIEWERS.

I understand that this is not usually considered a compliment, especially among those who claim to hate television. (See #2 above.) I am not one of those people. I love television. My television set ownership has been spotty over the last thirteen years, the length of *AFHV*'s run, for the same reason that I don't keep store-bought whipped cream in the house: It's not good for me, I love it, I have no shame, and I would consume it half the day if I had it, rolling around on my back like the dumb animal I am, TV and whipped cream both, possibly at the same time. Which is why the first thing I do when I get in a hotel room is try to find *America's Funniest Home Videos*. (It's a good thing they don't offer Reddi-wip in minibars.) They run the best episodes in the morning, by which I mean the ones with the original host, Bob Saget, upon whom I have a rather serious crush.

I *said* I had a problem.

In my defense I think that *AFHV* has been inadvertently conducting a long behavior-modification experiment on me: I watched *America's Funniest Home Videos*, I laughed out loud, I got suffused with endorphins, and then they showed me a picture of Bob Saget, and eventually I grew to associate Bob Saget with the pleasant afterglow of belly laughter. Plus he did some of the really lame voice-overs for some of the videos that entertained me so, like when an unsuspecting dachshund goes over to a garden hose just before someone turns it on: "Wow, it's hot, I'm one hot dog! What's this over here? It looks like . . . HOLY SHLAMOLEY!"

Etc.

There is no narrative, there are no characters, you never have to ask "Who's that?" or "Where did he come from?" You can watch any episode, any five minutes, and not feel left out of all the other episodes and minutes. It is a show that requires no devotion. Indeed, it does not even require an attention span. There are no morals. There is no pretense. There is not even a minimum IQ requirement.

I did once have a long conversation with a friend about a touching video with two small boys watching their father as Santa

Claus creep across the front yard. It led to a discussion of child-hood hopes and dreams. Happily I have forgotten the details.

It is an honest TV show: low budget, pandering, ridiculous.

4. No, but it's really funny.

It boils down to this: *America's Funniest Home Videos* is the only television show that reliably makes me laugh out loud. Anytime I have ever seen an episode, I end up with tears running down my face. Usually it's an intrepid-small-dog or cranky-kid video that does it, though I do like those tumbling senior citizens, because they always laugh when they sit up on the dance floor. I don't like the various blows to the groin, but they are, by their nature, over fast.

It makes me laugh. There have been times in my life—I'm not kidding about this—when I have been wretchedly unhappy about something, and that's when I actually look at the TV listings to see if and when *AFHV* is on. And things always seem a little better when I watch it, because no matter what, it will make me laugh. It won't erase my problems, but it sure as hell won't remind me of them.

There are television shows that have made me think, and television shows that have moved me to tears. Heck, there are television *commercials* that have moved me to tears. Forget 'em all.

Do I laugh because I am simple? Do I laugh because I am mean? The unexamined life is not worth living, says the philosopher, and yet the reason I love *America's Funniest Home Videos* is that it is a show that takes me out of myself in a way that art never does. Oh, I said I wouldn't mention art, and don't get me wrong: I'm not knocking the stuff. Here is a comparison of *America's Funniest Home Videos* to art: Compared to art, *America's Funniest*

Home Videos sucks. Art is moving and painful and funny and res-
onant and unsettling and essential and endlessly reaching and im-
proving and sometimes demoralizing. *America's Funniest Home
Videos* is none of these things.

Trapped on a desert island, of course, I'd want *Great Expecta-
tions*! Give me *Lolita* or *Citizen Kane* or a book of Breughel paint-
ings or a collection of Auden: Let me be reminded of how life is
going on without me, in its doggy way; let me think on the works
of man while out of sight of the people I love.

That is, if there is a chance I'll see them again.

But what if there isn't? What if I'm on that island forever, and
will never again be company to anyone? What if I am only ruined
by knowing that the complications of life are over for me? What if
all I have to look forward to is sand, and more sand, and the god-
damn relentless ocean that keeps the cities of the world from me?

Well then, give me *America's Funniest Home Videos*. Let me
drink deep of silliness and let it soften my brain, the bridal gowns
caught on fire, someone else's relatives embarrassing them; let us
see gravity, that practical joker, in its lightest mood, knocking
people down and letting them stand back up. Gravity is tragic,
too; gravity and nature probably landed me on this desert island,
but sometimes they have a sense of humor. Let me forgive gravity and nature. Let me laugh at tobogganists and their head-on
collisions and beachcombers walloped by waves.

And let me gaze upon the laughing audience in any one of
AFHV's many, many reaction shots. The audience is free, the audience is in civilization, and yet here we are, they and I, doing the
same thing, paralyzed by laughter, utterly uncivilized by that
tabby, that toddler, that dancing, fumbling zaftig uncle. We are all
of us earnest. Earnestness can be the deepest of pleasures.

I love that uncle—I love him earnestly, sincerely—though I
know nothing about him, except that he's laughing, too.

DAYS OF OUR LIVES

Susan Perabo

"I'm never watching again!"

This from my grandmother, who over the last several years of her life phoned me at least once a month with the same furious declaration. She'd call me as the credits went swimming up the screen, past that ever-filling, ever-draining hourglass. "They've gone too far this time. Don't you think?"

("Too far"—i.e., the third bout of amnesia in two years, the alcoholic paraplegic's onset of hysterical blindness, the baby switched at birth, then immediately kidnapped, etc.)

"So this is it?" I'd say. "You're just going to cut yourself off, cold turkey?"

Pause. Sigh. I imagine her in the embrace of her tan recliner, the weary creak of the springs as she rocks forward to take hold of the re-mote. The credits have ended; now it's an ad for Pampers, Pine-Sol, Hamburger Helper, some household product expected to sell well at this hour. The afternoon stretches out before her only as far as the things within arm's reach: the large-print Agatha Christie, the tube of Pringles, the pad and pencil, the telephone, the remote control.

"All right," she'd say. "I'll wait and see how this one thing turns out. But then, Sue, that's it!"

⌷ ⌷ ⌷

In 1965, when *Days of Our Lives* premiered on NBC, my grand-mother was sixty-two, my mother twenty-six, and I four years from being born. LBJ was starting to work up a sweat. The moon was unspoiled. On TV, *The Andy Griffith Show* was beginning its sixth year in the top ten.

Enter the Hortons, Tom and Alice and their five adult children: Mickey, Marie, Addie, Bill, and Tommy. This family is the center of *Days of Our Lives*; for the next forty years and beyond, all plots will spool out from them. When the show begins, the children are all in their twenties, embarking on adulthood with big dreams and wobbly knees. Soon, Tommy will go to Vietnam. Marie will become a nun. Mickey and Bill will begin their lifelong battle over women. Addie will marry, have a daughter, and one day in those first couple of seasons, a car will veer out of control and speed toward Addie and her baby and Addie will sacrifice her life to push the carriage out of the way. In the carriage: Hope.

Today, Hope is nearing forty; the sands in her hourglass have dwindled at approximately the same rate as the sands in mine. True, her forty years have been considerably fuller—she has been kidnapped nearly a dozen times, suffered from several bouts of amnesia, and was once lowered into a bubbling vat of acid—but we are nonetheless peers and have been for my entire life. Assuming she retains her uncanny ability to cheat death, I fully expect Hope and I will grow old together.

⌷ ⌷ ⌷

You can probably imagine the crap I've taken as a result of my devotion to *Days of Our Lives*. For years I've weathered ridicule from serious writer types, friends and colleagues who, upon learning my dirty little secret, feel it necessary to reevaluate me. Sure, we've all had TV periods we're not proud of—the year we watched *Who's the Boss?* every night over dinner, the summer when *Melrose Place* loomed large—but *Days of Our Lives* is my longtime companion, not something that can be chalked up to poverty or gin or even a crisis of faith. I don't watch it every day (real life intervenes), but on average I catch it at least once a week. So, my perplexed friends ask, what kind of intelligent person, a writer of literary fiction, a professor of English, could possibly choose to spend even a moment of her busy life following the preposterous adventures of clichéd characters in Salem, USA, a town so wholly implausible that it shudders every time a door slams?

Part of it, of course, is pure nostalgia, the same kind of nostalgia that makes bad music from the seventies and eighties seem so great to us now that we're approaching middle age. It's not that those Styx songs are actually any good; it's that they remind us of being crammed in a sticky, smoky backseat with six other fifteen-year-olds. So it is with *Days*; the show reminds me of the people who watched it with me, of my best friend in college, who referred to Hope as Thunder Thighs during her brief foray into professional figure skating, or of my grandmother, who watched a teenaged Hope make out with the rebellious Bo and asked me, horrified, "Do people really kiss that way?"

But if that were all of it—the nostalgia factor—it wouldn't be enough to keep me watching. The fact is, the show can be pretty terrible. The dialogue is often eardrum piercing. Many of the characters have silly names. Everyone wears too much makeup, and it's always perfectly applied, even after sex or emergency surgery. There are more coincidences in a single summer than Charles Dickens concocted over his entire career. Then there's my grandmother's gripe: *This time they've gone too far.* And indeed they had—Marlena possessed by the devil; Julie Olson Banning Anderson Williams's eventual marriage to her own stepfather (Hope's dad, Addie's widower); Carly buried alive and listening to her own "funeral" through a microphone installed in her casket by the woman who buried her; the computer chip implanted, de-planted, and replanted in John's head; Kate's stolen embryo; Hope's look-alike evil princess; Stefano's tenth resurrection after certain death. These outrageous story lines are why it's so easy to write off *Days,* to dismiss—and diss—the soap opera in general. On the surface (and there's a whole lot of surface) soaps are nothing more than silly, harmless distraction.

But listen. Here is a secret. The soap opera is in fact an art form unlike any other, an entertainment unparalleled in contemporary society. The irony is that the very elements about soaps that are most often ridiculed are actually the elements that make them completely and brilliantly unique. "How can you watch that show?" people always say to me. "It's so unrealistic." For years I grinned shamefully, shrugged, went through all the appropriate gestures of disgrace, mumbling something about my grandmother and tradition. But no longer. Finally setting aside my awkward rationalizations long enough to see the truth, I have come to this shocking, soap-affirming realization: In several significant ways, *Days of Our Lives* is not unrealistic at all. In fact, it may well be more realistic than any other work of art we have ever known. Why?

It keeps going.

That's it. That hourglass never runs out. There is no conclusion, no resolution. There is only conflict and rising action. Plots do not end; they fold themselves into other plots, spastically veer in other directions. There's always someone leaving with high hopes or a broken heart, someone returning with short hair or a better boyfriend, someone claiming *This is forever,* someone vowing not to make the same mistake again. Parents, siblings, lovers, and friends—no matter where they go—all resurface eventually, either to save the day or screw things up completely. If this sounds familiar, it is. Indeed, no medium has ever captured the immense and infuriating scope of real life quite like the soap opera. This is why my grandmother could never stop watching; each time she stuck around to see "how this one thing turns out," another three things were starting to get interesting. *Days of Our Lives,* like life, exhibits no definable arc of story, just an endless series of fits and starts.

To make a long story longer, my grandmother used to say, of her own stories, five minutes and three tangents into what she had promised would be a brief foray into the past. I never minded, of course. (Okay, that's probably a bit of revisionist history—I probably minded when I was eleven, probably got bored and wished we could get back to our card game.) Her stories took forever to get where they were going—and sometimes never got there at all. But those kinds of stories are usually the best stories, because they're the ones that mimic the way we really live. In real life, we almost never get where we think we're going when we think we're going to, and when we finally do arrive, we're so changed by what's happened along the way that even the destination itself is altered. Such it is for me, such it was for my grandmother, and such it remains for every major character on *Days of Our Lives.* On prime-time TV, boy meets girl/boy loses girl/boy gets girl often happens in an hour, sometimes even in a half hour. In many renowned prime-time dramas a character is diagnosed with cancer one week, then spends the next episode on his deathbed and the next being lowered in the ground. Ah, if only we were all so efficient with our own demise. Soaps recognize the truth: Love and death take for-freaking-ever.

This trait, the for-freaking-ever factor, guarantees that soap characters make the same mistakes repeatedly, go down the same roads again and again despite the multiple flashing DANGER signs that line the pavement. Bits of dialogue that usually indicate upcoming disaster include:

1. "But he's changed."
2. "But she's changed."
3. "But I've changed."

Rarely true in life, rarely true in soaps. It's not that the characters never change—they just never change *much*. How many times have I heard Hope say, "I know I should stay here where I'm not in immediate and terrible danger, but darn it, I want to be in on the action"? (This is why she gets kidnapped so often . . . and what ultimately led to that vat of acid.) All the Hortons suffer from this terrible inability to learn; Bill and Mickey have gone so far as to shoot each other over women, despite the fact that the women never wind up being worth the trouble. Marie was tempted from the nunnery again and again by the same sleazy guy. Even Alice— now too old to make really bad mistakes in her own life—sits at her kitchen table doling out doughnuts and lame advice to her children, grandchildren, and great-grandchildren. Don't these people ever learn? But wait—when have *you* ever learned? I wonder . . . could this be why so many people hate soaps so much? Could it be that, hiding behind nitpicky criticisms about plot devices and silly names, what those who dismiss soaps truly fear is that the characters on them are as stupid, and stupid in frighteningly authentic ways, as the rest of us? That what we want is not reality at all (though we literary types clamor for it) but characters who actually learn from their mistakes, and who—moments after a mistake, a thimble of reflection later—are able to change themselves into the kinds of people they wish themselves to be?

⌐ ⌐ ⌐

When my grandmother died in 1993, I adopted Alice Horton as my pretend grandmother. The actress who plays Alice, Frances Reid, has been on the show since that very first episode thirty-nine years ago. She and John Clarke, who plays her son Mickey, are the two remaining cast members from that first season; all of the current characters, though many have been recast, are part or kin of, or friend to, that original group. There's a haunting kind of continuity about this, a continuity that is totally unique to the long-running soap opera. No matter how many times you've seen each episode of *Andy Griffith*, the fact remains: It's over. Imagine that show—*Days'* contemporary in the mid-sixties—having lasted nearly forty years. Imagine Ron Howard as Opie, having grown up, grown old, with you. Imagine following Dorothy through the days and years after she dreams of Oz. Imagine following Holden Caulfield into adulthood. Even comic-book characters, some of whom have lasted nearly a century, don't count because they don't age. Superman is always thirtysomething; Little Orphan Annie will never hit puberty.

Strangest of all—disconcerting to some, comforting to others—is that the haunting continuity of long-running soaps is more dependable even than your actual life. *Days of Our Lives* is on every single weekday on every single NBC affiliate in the country, making it more consistently accessible to me than any friend, family member, partner, or pet I have ever had. More important? Of course not. But a solace nonetheless, for in forty years I'll be in my own recliner. I'll have my large-print books and my Pringles and my telephone, perhaps even with a granddaughter on the other end. And on TV, or whatever I'm watching in 2045? Hope, her hair gray, her face lined, her frail body in the kitchen chair her grandmother Alice used to occupy. And a story that continues to unfold.

THE TRIBE HAS SPOKEN

Phyllis Rose

A workaday boat bounces through heavy seas in the South Pacific. Sixteen Americans, men and women, most in their twenties and thirties, a few older, hang on anxiously. One throws up in a bucket. Miles from land, two life rafts are hurled into the water. The people hit the water one by one, roll aboard the rafts, and start paddling. Each raft hauls behind it a box filled with essential supplies: a knife, two machetes, two pots, a frying pan, a magnifying glass, and two containers for water. Two teams of *Survivor* contestants are heading for separate beaches on the Marquesa Islands, where they will live, with no food supplied them, for the next thirty-nine days. The teams will meet periodically to compete in games and contests that sometimes produce a reward for winners (food, for example, or contact with loved ones) and sometimes a punishment for the losers: The losing team has to meet in "tribal council" and vote out one of its members. Every TV hour ends with someone being voted off the island, until only two are left. Then a jury, composed of the last seven people to be eliminated, picks one of the two as winner of the million-dollar prize. Evidently this is more a test of social skills than survival skills, and the texture of the show, with everyone in a small community observing and commenting on everyone else, is closer to Jane Austen than to Joseph Conrad, despite the Conradian settings.

In their bathing suits and straw hats, keyed up at the start of the competition, not yet malnourished and sleep-deprived, the contestants all seem to be working like maniacs paddling the rafts. Still the rafts move slowly. One man, older than the rest, complains that they don't seem to be getting anywhere and admits he's exhausted. But at last, first one raft makes it to shore (the Rotu team) and then the other (Maraamu). Rotu lets out whoops of triumph, gathers in a huddle to hug. On the other beach, cheers are more hollow. Resentments are already festering.

One of the female contestants has a fabulous body. Her large, taut-skinned, perfectly shaped breasts are decorated rather than covered by her bikini top. These too-good-to-be-true boobs belong to Sarah, an "account manager" from California, and Sean, a young African-American teacher identified as coming from "Harlem," has taken an instant dislike to Sarah because of them. Footage of Maraamu's paddling to the beach has Sean's voice-over commentary: "As we were coming in that maybe last fifty yards or so, we all made a concerted effort to make it to land. It was quite evident that Sarah wasn't doing anything at all." The footage, zooming in on Sarah, backs him up: Her paddle idle, she shouts, "Kick! Kick! Good! Good!" to the guys in the water pushing the back of the raft.

In debriefing interviews after each event, contestants face the camera and comment on the action and on other participants, producing some monologues of a candid bitchiness hardly matched outside of *Richard III.* Perhaps because they are filmed alone on a remote island facing only a TV camera, the contestants seem unaware that millions of people will hear what they say: They seem to speak their most secret thoughts. From these monologues editors cut pieces of commentary to run over the footage of the unfolding events. It is painstaking editorial work but worth it.

Sean seems actually to allude to Shakespeare's famous image of Cleopatra ("The barge she sat in, like a burnished throne / Burned on the water") as he continues to skewer Sarah. "Sarah's arrival was almost like Cleopatra. It was like the servants are paddling and lifting, and she's sitting on the crate looking so 'marvelous' [modelesque?], with her boobs hanging out and her goldilocks in the air." His resentment is riveting, and the camera supports the accuracy of what he claims. Sarah does swan it over everyone else, standing up like a queen while the others work, majestically lofting her breasts into the wind, as the raft comes ashore. Sean, that hot-headed bundle of bitterness, is allowed, by excellent editing, by state-of-the-art and expensive documentary techniques, to shine as a narrative artist.

This is why I love *Survivor*. The people speak, not the usual pieties of the evening news and athletic events, about going in there and doing their best, and taking it one thing at a time, and just having a good time no matter the outcome, and seeking closure, and doing it for their dead and dying loved ones, and being proud to be this and finding strength to do that, but good, bitchy, biased-filled, bigotry-shaped, minute-by-minute put-downs of other people's behavior.

Everyone observes everyone else. Everyone comments on everyone else. Spontaneous human interaction has never, to my knowledge, been so closely scrutinized on prime-time TV. Instant playback, instant commentary, as though this were the Super Bowl and every offside kick or touchdown were replayed and subjected to the players' comments, as well as the announcers'. Cameramen and soundmen work twenty-four hours a day to sweep up every scrap that emerges from the contestants' subconscious. Thirteen hours of television are distilled from more than a thousand hours of tape. People who used to work as writers are now hired to watch the tedious raw footage, on the lookout for moments of meaning and drama. The result is not "reality," a word I hardly ever use outside quotation marks. It is unscripted, semi-spontaneously occurring human drama whittled into narrative interest by master craftsmen.

ᗡ ᗡ ᗡ

Although, by convention, a tribe hates to vote anyone out, the truth is that in the early sessions they're eager to. The first episodes show strangers getting to know one another, feeling out sympathies, and deciding whom they cannot bear. Who will be the first one voted off? Whom do Americans dislike most? As we will see, they do not like the bossy. They hate being told what to do. They do not like the old, especially if they are also bossy, and thus remind young contestants of their parents. They do not like loud people, though few are capable of silence. But what they distance themselves from most immediately is craziness. Anyone suspected of being odd is the first to go.

Is Sean crazy? He's definitely emotional and deeply religious. We see him rolling around on the sand just after the craft beaches, in his happiness to be back on land. He had never been on water. "When we first arrived on land," he explained, "it was beyond land. I'm emotional when I think of the miracles God has performed." Boats are a miracle. Land is a miracle. Their safe arrival is a miracle in which God has played a direct part. "His hand was under the raft." He grabs Peter, the curly-haired, wide-eyed bowling alley owner, and standing knee-deep in water, holding hands, they offer thanks to God for their deliverance.

Rob, an unsmiling, down-to-earth construction worker from Massachusetts, comments on the hand-holding couple: "Either they are playing the game real early or they are off their rockers." Chunky Rob, with his broad Boston accent, is totally missing the love-thy-neighbor gene, but sometimes he seems on the mark. Soon we see footage of Peter lying back on the sand talking to his teammates about the nose, the eyes, the ears, the mouth, how we pee, how we shit, how we must be aware of all the orifices in our body to really understand ourselves. Rob says, "He looks like a normal guy, but he's going on and on about being holy and I'm thinking he's talking about, like, spiritualness, but he's talking about actual holes in your body. He's a fruit loop."

The fruit loop goes. At tribal council that night, Maraamu, which lost the immunity challenge—a boat race—sits around the sacred fire, each person's torch lit. All the tribe members walk up to a voting booth/confessional and write on a piece of paper the name of the person they are voting to expel. Each one gives a reason. Sometimes the camera shows the vote and reveals the reason. Often not, depending on how the producers want to build the tension.

Sean, true to his instinctive distaste, votes for (that is, against) Sarah: "Other than having two floating devices that can help us out there, what value is she to the group? The more males, the better you can survive." Others are more indulgent about Sarah's body. Vepecia, called Vee, an African-American office manager from Oregon, says, "Sarah has a very cute body. She paid a lot for it. And if you have it, of course flaunt it." Patricia, a truck assembler from South Carolina, gets some votes because she's old (forty-nine). But Peter gets the most votes. In Sarah's words, "He has this strange smirk. He's just strange."

The exile's symbolic torch is extinguished. "The tribe has spoken," the emcee intones. Peter, like everyone expelled from para-

dise after him, tries to hide his feelings and make a plucky exit.
He has said on camera that he never felt comfortable in this group
from the moment the boat landed, and aside from practicing yoga
and paying a lot of attention to breathing—the source of his di-
sastrous monologue on holes—he doesn't seem strange at all. The
official *Survivor* website reveals that he graduated summa cum
laude from Boston College, lives with his wife and children in a
house his father built, and co-owns the bowling alley and a wine
shop with his brother.

No, the real fruit loop—as I see it, an adorable fruit loop—is
on the other team. Under Gabe's innocuous all-American desig-
nation, "Bartender," lies a hippie counterculturist of singular pu-
rity. His angelic blond curls and round metal eyeglasses suggest a
student more than a bartender, as does his frustrated-idealist bleat
in reply to a teammate's exhortations to make fire, find water, and
build shelter. According to Gabe (and he says this with considerable passion), they have more important things to do. More
important than fire, water, and shelter? What would that be? Getting to know one another. "Stop going off by yourself," he tells
Kathy, the real-estate agent from Vermont who has been trying to
find food and is now urging her teammates to build a hut and ac-
cusing them of inaction. "We're trying to be a society. There is a
lot going on here. I want to get to know you more than I want a
shelter." (Shot of Kathy, incredulous.) Gabe, as will become clear
in the short time he is allotted on the island, is not there to win a
million dollars. He is there to build a new and better world as a
model for mankind. That he frankly says he does not want to "play
the game" and is not interested in the money makes him untrustworthy in the eyes of his teammates, who seem genuinely puzzled
by his utopian rap, and he will be the first person voted off Rotu.

When you find out more about the contestants, which is easy
to do by going to one of the many websites devoted to them, you

see how much selection—that is, narrative art—is involved merely in the terse on-screen identification of each contestant. Sean, identified as "from Harlem," actually lives and works in Los Angeles, and, given that he majored in theater and psychology at SUNY Albany, may well have acting aspirations, although he is currently a junior-high-school teacher. Gabe, according to the official CBS website, "was born and raised in the tiny alternative community of Celo, North Carolina. His father is a doctor and his mother is a nurse. In addition, they run a small farm with goats, chickens, rabbits, and fields of blueberry bushes." Gabe has been at various times a professional figure skater, a cellist, a student of jazz and ballet, a leader of student adventure trips in Europe, a hiker of the Appalachian Trail, a student at the University of North Carolina, and a French science fiction major at another college where students get no grades and teach themselves. Currently he prepares students for the math SATs while he drives a car for an elderly gentleman and occasionally bartends in Hollywood, although his on-screen ID lists Celo, North Carolina, as his "hometown."

So the geographical diversity of the group is somewhat constructed. Sean and Gabe, although labeled "teacher from Harlem" and "bartender from North Carolina," could just as easily be called Southern Californians with backgrounds in performance. Vecepia, too, although she is "from" Oregon, currently lives in California, as does Hunter, the pilot.

Sean's theatrical streak makes for great TV, so he gets a lot of airtime. He especially relishes presenting himself as "a Malcolm X, militant-type brother" (Vecepia's words), which brings racial issues onto prime-time television in an unusually explicit way. Footage in an early episode shows him and Vee sitting on a log chatting happily, and Sean says in voice-over, "Me and her playing a whole 'nother game that they don't even know—that when you're a person of color, and you're the only one, you have to play—and that's something they don't even have to worry about. See, everybody can just be themselves. We have to be ourselves but then hold back a little bit. On top of that she believes in God and I believe in God. And we're bound by Christ and that's a stronger bond, stronger than race, stronger than anything." This is such a powerful statement that the producers have to go a very long time without ever showing us Vecepia and Sean together again, lest we conclude they have formed an unbreakable alliance. As it is, we see Sean chilling with Rob, or Rob, lying next to Sarah, telling us she will do whatever he tells her to do, or Rob, alone, talking to the camera, revealing his belief that he controls all the action. Vecepia, a mild, unself-dramatizing, sensible woman, we rarely see.

Maraamu does terribly in the first three episodes, losing the two rewards challenges (snorkel gear is the reward for the first, blankets, pillows, and lanterns for the second) and the first three immunity challenges. Three times they have to go to tribal council and vote someone off. The atmosphere in the group is poisonous, and you're not surprised they don't win. But in fact, they haven't lost by as much as you would think from the way they're presented. For example, in the third episode the tribes are given the task of building a raft out of bamboo poles ferried to the beaches. Footage shows Maraamu team members looking at the poles hopelessly, arguing about how to build the raft, getting nowhere fast, while Rotu is shown springing into action, praising the team member who comes up with the design, working together efficiently to get the thing built. Yet, although no narrative point is made of it, both crafts are ready on time, neither functions appreciably better than the other, and the winners win by less than a length—so it's hard to see in their triumph anything more than luck, though it's presented as the result of teamwork.

Maraamu has a natural leader in Hunter, a former navy pilot, currently a pilot for FedEx. Vecepia, asked by the emcee, Jeff, at the first tribal council whether a leader has emerged in their group, says yes, Hunter is their leader and she wouldn't have it any other way, because the guy knows what he's doing. This is the kind of clean-cut, unflappable, competent man you're happy to have flying your plane. From the moment of their arrival, he's the one who knows things. He knows how much sunlight they have left and how to use the magnifying glass to make fire. He understands the prevailing winds and predicts the weather. From the get-go, Sean mocks him, calling him the Helicopter Weatherman, issuing parody orders in his voice to gather banana leaves to "funnel the nutrients" for tomorrow's breakfast. It's funny, but in a monologue direct to the audience, Sean says, "I'm an alpha male, too. So I find it hard to just follow someone blindly like my daddy." Later Sean's resistance to whoever tries to get him to work is cast in political and racial terms: "I feel like we're doing too much labor on this island. Definitely feel like the master is watching. I'm, like, slavery's been over."

The camera continues to show exasperation and dissension in the ranks of Maraamu. Hunter is exasperated with Sarah, who seems to feel she's on a vacation, and with Sean, who doesn't pull his weight. Gina, a nature guide from Florida, agrees with Hunter. "Sean seems so strong physically, you think he's gonna do this and that, but he's lazy." Footage shows Sean floating on his back in a life vest (he doesn't swim well) singing a song, while Hunter cracks coconuts with a machete. Boy, am I with Gina and Hunter. Sean and Rob and Sarah are driving me nuts. I don't know which one I want gone first. Hunter and Gina vote to oust Sarah, the useless one. But Patricia, the competent truck assembler (in fact, she is as much a "cosmetologist" as a truck assembler, according to the website), the senior citizen of forty-nine, who, as she has relaxed into the group, has asked to be called Momma and has gotten a bit more officious, is the one voted off. "The mom thing is getting old," says Vee.

Everyone in Maraamu is mad at everyone else. Sarah knows Hunter and Gina voted against her, and she attacks them. They didn't even bother to wake her up that morning. If they wanted her to work, they should have woken her up. Sean is angry, too, and mouths off about "disrespect." Hunter asked him to go get water, and it has been festering. Does Sean mean, Hunter asks, that he doesn't want to work for the tribe? Sean says no, he's willing to work, but Hunter "told" him to get the water. He didn't ask. "It was the way you said it." Hunter's method of communication is disrespectful, according to Sean. This in turn exasperates Gina. "Sarah and Sean—they don't want you to ask them to do anything. They think they should know how to do it. And if you ask them, they're going to get pissed off. I don't know what kind of communication they want. Maybe telecommunication?"

At the start of a new *Survivor*, a certain kind of contestant is eager to prove that he or she can build a fire, make huts, gather taro, catch fish, haul water, weave thatch. Just as certainly there is another kind of contestant who resents all this bustle as officious showing off or nagging coercion. On the other team, Rotu, Kathy, the real-estate agent, is playing the Hunter role and just as certainly is resented for it. (According to Gabe, "Kathy slips easily into the role of being skipper. But we don't need a skipper.") Kathy, smarter than Hunter in this regard, learns she has to play down her own competence and leadership instincts. She kisses and hugs more than usual. She shows vulnerability. She is willing to make a fool of herself. When John, spearfishing, lands his hand on a sea urchin and picks up a dozen needles in his fingers, he knows the antidote is urine (he's a registered nurse) and stumbles ashore begging someone to pee on his hand. Kathy steps right up to the plate. While the others look aghast, John's pain is immediately relieved and he comments afterward: "It could have been peroxide. I didn't think it was weird she was squatting with my hand between her legs." (To some viewers this sequence may answer a question that's been hanging in the air: Is John gay?)

That night, Hunter is voted off Maraamu. It took me completely by surprise, and I was horrified. Those creeps, useless Sarah, blustering Rob, resentful Sean—who does he remind me of?—have gotten together and voted off the most competent person on their team. It's a triumph of the nasty and small-minded over the large and community-spirited, the incompetent over the competent. There is no justice! What a lesson.

But the more I think of it, the more the lesson changes. This is democracy. The useless and bitter, the surgically enhanced and the delusional, the lazy and the worker bees, all have a vote. They have the right to see events according to their own lights. In this unscripted situation, each contestant goes into action drawing on the scripts and scraps of scripts they carry in their heads, wherever they come from—the Boy Scouts, Sunday school, gangster movies, slave narratives, or self-help columns. Gina and Hunter share a script that I find congenial: Take charge, work hard, get the job done, whatever the job is. This is not a vacation. Pitch in. Cooperate. But Sean, I realize, has a more subversive—and actually, a more interesting—script in his head. Who does he remind me of? Ah, yes, it's Caliban, and, damn it, he is not hauling water for Prospero. In fact, he's going to vote Prospero off the island. Who said it was Prospero's island, anyway? (Sean's version: "I refuse to sit back and watch the golden boy make suggestions.") As for Rob, he's been watching Mafia movies: "Everybody wants to be the big man. So the smart man will sit back and let everybody else be the big man and bank on their mistakes."

What schadenfreude this show provides—that joy you're not supposed to have when things go wrong for other people. Your pleasure when they're voted off, when the camera reveals them doing something silly, when they make themselves obnoxious, when they're shrill or bossy or condescending or self-satisfied. Your pleasure as they itch from bugs and wake up wet from rain and slog through the jungle carrying a silly six-foot torch and eat the same uninteresting messes day after day and listen to the inane chatter of their teammates and not be other than interested and caring. You, thank the Lord, are not there. You are home in a queen-sized bed with your husband, in a heated or air-cooled house, with the dog at your feet and a refrigerator stocked with fruit, cheese, and wine, and a telephone next to the bed to call your best friends, should you feel like talking to them and be able to locate them on their cell phones. From *Your Show of Shows* to *Northern Exposure* and beyond, television has gone to great pains to create on-screen communities of which one wants to be a part. Each member of the precinct, hospital ward, or legal firm is colorful, quirky, appealing. They all work so beautifully together. Each is so necessary to the effect of the whole. What a breath of fresh air, then, to turn on *Survivor* and see some people who make you want to run in the other direction, glad to be in your own home, with your chosen companions, and your well-stocked kitchen, and a lock on the front gate, and the right to refuse invitations to tribal councils—people who work better together the fewer of them there are. It's a very specialized kind of escapism that wafts you to a Pacific island for an hour and leaves you feeling happy you aren't there.

As the teams shrink, week by week, sometimes symmetrically,

sometimes with a wild imbalance, the rules of the game change and so can the composition of the teams. In the fourth episode of *Survivor*, "Marquesas," a random realignment puts Sean, Vecepia, and Rob onto the hitherto-successful Rotu and takes Neleh, Paschal, and Kathy away to join Sarah and Gina on a greatly altered Maraamu. Neleh (pronounced "Nuh-LEE-a"), a sweet, conflict-avoiding twenty-one-year-old Mormon studying to be a makeup artist, and Paschal, a kindly judge living in a small town in Georgia, have taken to each other like father and daughter. Both work hard and never complain. They spread happiness wherever they go. Gina, who surely would have been booted off the old Maraamu right after Hunter, now finds herself with congenial company. She and her new teammates quickly get rid of Sarah (without Rob, she has no defender) and make a formidable team, winning several important challenges, even at half the size of the other tribe.

Always, at some point a "merge" takes place, and the remnants of the two initially eight-person teams become one team. That can be good news for the team that is larger going into the merge. They can then pick off the others week by week until they are forced to turn on one another. But sometimes the merge results in a completely new mix and new friendships ("alliances" in *Survivor*-speak). Some people race around trying to make new alliances, but the deeper people understand that this is not really negotiable and remain true to their instinctive bonds, as Neleh and Paschal do, as it turns out Vecepia and Sean do.

The eighth person voted off and each succeeding one become part of a seven-member "jury" that chooses between the last two survivors. It's a flat-out popularity contest, often between two people, neither of whom is liked. In the very first *Survivor* season, the two final contestants were Richard Hatch, a gay management consultant who was close to no one but whose style of "playing the game" everyone respected, and Kelly Wigglesworth, a young female rafting guide who had closely befriended and then betrayed at least one other contestant. A few members of the jury were quite open about their dislike of both finalists and said that Hatch, the eventual winner, was merely the lesser of two evils. Susan Hawk, a feisty truck driver and the swing voter, hated Wigglesworth, whom she thought had betrayed her. Hawk made a wild and whirring speech about evil, saying that one of the finalists was a rat and the other a snake. In nature the snake eats the rat. Therefore she was voting for (that is, *for*) Hatch. Very few scripted TV shows can rise above the writers' own good taste, intelligence, social timidity, and respect for convention to come up with moments like that!

The finale of the Marquesas season was not so dramatic. Sean, amazingly, made it to the final five but then was voted off, leaving three women, Kathy, Vecepia, and Neleh, and the other man, Paschal. At this point, the challenges produce personal, not team, immunity, and it becomes very important to win it. Vecepia won the next immunity challenge, a quiz based on contestants' knowledge of the events of the game and of others' lives—exactly the kind of thing Vecepia was good at. She had chosen as her "luxury" item a book to write in and had quietly recorded events on the island as they took place. A tie, two votes against Neleh, two against Kathy, threw the decision of who should leave next to a lottery, which Paschal lost. He seemed happy to sacrifice himself for the sake of Neleh. As it turned out, he was on his last legs, physically, and collapsed from dehydration that night.

Kathy lost the final immunity challenge. Neleh and Vecepia brokered a deal and became the final two. There was no speech against them as vicious as the one Susan Hawk had made against

Kelly Wigglesworth, but Tammy, a journalist from Arizona, said that neither of these women should have won. She resented their "holier-than-thou" attitude.

I was glad she'd said it. I hoped my husband and I weren't the only ones cringing when days began with Neleh-led prayer meetings and when Vecepia, entering the final round, alluded to the life of Christ: "And Christ said while he was hanging on the cross, 'It is finished, it is almost done.'"

The genre has come to be known as "reality TV," but "unscripted TV drama" is more accurate, "broadly scripted and meticulously edited TV drama" more accurate still. By choosing the initial sixteen contestants, by fixing the location and deciding what food and tools are available to the contestants, by setting the rules and creating the reward and the immunity challenges, the producers broadly script the action. But mostly they create the drama through the editing. The basic mechanism of narrative art, whether fiction or nonfiction, cinema or literature, is the selection and arrangements of details. Andy Warhol kept a camera trained for hours on the Empire State Building and called it a feature film. He shot another of a person smoking a cigarette. He was making a point about art and "reality." True-reality TV would be unbroken footage of sand, ocean, people sitting around being bored, thinking their own thoughts, nothing happening. To produce watchable film demands selection and arrangement. No one would turn on their TV to see six days of bank-security-camera footage of people moving toward the tellers, even if there was a bank robbery on the seventh.

"Real life" produces great moments, but inefficiently, compared to art, the great condenser. And as for story lines, they aren't visible in daily life. The struggles of one contestant, the friendship of others—these are all creations by elimination from the great mass of anarchic and fundamentally boring experience. Depending on which moments get shown, the producers can, of course, build sympathy for a contestant or make him look absolutely terrible. Tin-pot Machiavellis face the camera and confide their belief that they are absolutely essential and their position impregnable moments before they are voted into nonentity. We are let in on strategies that fly in the face of everything we know. We get to witness behavior that only complete self-absorption would think was cute. The young scoff the old. The straight scoff the gay. Sophisticates scoff the rural. Agnostics scoff the pious. The pious ask for forgiveness for having lied and praise their faith in God's mercy. A grown person walks to the water's edge and hurls into the air a shriek of anger and self-pity you might expect in a child. Little details tell the story, and someone chooses those details.

As a literary critic and nonfiction writer, I am fascinated by the fine line between "lie" and "manipulation" on the one hand and "art" on the other. But most Americans do not see life or even reality TV as a literary construct. Some *Survivor* contestants are amazingly naive about the degree of selection and arrangement involved in any act of representation. They expect the show to be utterly unbiased, that is, to present them exactly as they see themselves. They expect the producers' and editors' hands to be invisible.

Dirk Been, a participant in the first *Survivor,* wrote a letter to the show's producer, Mark Burnett, complaining that the experience had been "tainted" for him by Burnett's manipulations. His accusations were vague and unsupported: Burnett had expressed opinions and he had "swept things under the rug." "If you decide to do another show," Been wrote the producer, "you have to be 100 percent honest with all the contestants all of the time. Make sure they are aware that it is not going to be all 'reality.'" The contestants ought to be told, the letter continued, that "making good

TV is more important to you than being honest and true to themselves." What does that mean exactly? Is Been asking Burnett to make clear that he values the making of a good TV show more than he does being honest and true to the contestants? More than he cares about the contestants' being honest and true to themselves? More than he cares about helping the contestants to be honest and true to themselves? Who does he think this guy is? A TV producer? A shaper of souls? A pastor? God? Do we have any evidence that God himself cares more about encouraging people to be honest and true to themselves than he does about a good show?

Dirk Been's letter concludes, "I hope you don't think I'm a whining, sore loser. I just want to believe my experience was completely real."

Real. You would think that if a contestant on *Survivor* learned anything, it would be the constructed nature of reality. Certainly it's hard to feel sorry for someone who has agreed—in releases every would-be survivor must sign—to be filmed and taped twenty-four hours a day, seven days a week, with visible or hidden cameras, who is advised that the material so produced can be edited, cut, rearranged, adapted, dubbed, and otherwise modified at the producer's discretion, and who explicitly grants the producer the right to reveal information about him of a "personal, private, intimate, surprising, defamatory, disparaging, embarrassing, or unfavorable nature, that may be factual and/or fictional," and to present or portray him in a way that may expose him to "public ridicule, humiliation, and condemnation."

Is reality TV real? As real as the evening news, anyway. And to my mind it's a better way to find out about the state of our country, its resentments, its anxieties, its myths, its piety, its narcissism, its energy, its decadence, its idealism, its resilience and lack of it.

Only the best-written and -acted of current shows, like *The Sopranos,* come close to matching the entertainment and information value of *Survivor.* For the rest, I agree with a fan of reality shows who was quoted in the *New York Times*: "These real people, they're just crazy. They're a lot more interesting to watch than what writers are coming up with."

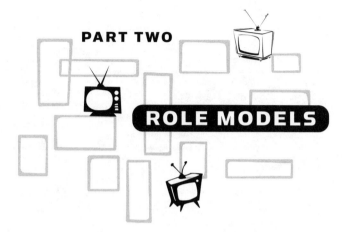

PART TWO

ROLE MODELS

FATHER KNOWS BEST

Susan Cheever

Even back then, on the day television arrived at our little house in the suburbs in the winter of 1957, I knew it would change everything. As a teenager, I preferred to live other people's lives; my own just wasn't interesting. I was one of those kids who read books by flashlight under the covers after bedtime, entranced by everything from Thornton Burgess tales about Little Joe Otter and Old Mother West Wind to Wilkie Collins's Victorian thriller *The Woman in White*. I didn't care, as long as the story took me away from our dumpy suburban home with its wall sconces and overstuffed couch and Danish modern furniture and obligatory family dinners. Books were my knights in shining armor, whisking me away from my humdrum and oppressed life as quickly and surely as the prince at the end of one of my favorite stories.

I spent as many evenings as possible sitting in the back of the old Victoria Theater in Ossining, New York, with my friend Sarah, who lived down the street. We saw *The Bridge on the River Kwai* and *Court Jester* with Danny Kaye. Dwight D. Eisenhower was president. We liked Ike, but we loved Elvis. We could sing all the words to "Hound Dog" and "Blue Suede Shoes." Somehow I knew that television would transcend all this. I had heard about a new kind of show called situation comedy, a show that would let me imagine ordinary lives, lives that were like ours, only make-believe, lives with none of the frictions and angers and money problems that seemed to be as much a part of our family as my two younger brothers.

The day the set finally came, I was at school. Did I mention that I hated school? I got home to find a small rectangular black box crowned with long, adjustable antennae resting on a wrought-iron cocktail table near the sofa. There it was, the Emerson, named appropriately after the father of modern philosophy. Its grainy black-and-white magic window was every bit as amazing as I expected. My father switched it on and, presto, I was sliding my slender foot into the glass slipper. There were the Mouske-teers, and Ed Sullivan, and the old comedians Milton Berle and Red Skelton. Of all the television shows on all three networks, the one that fascinated me was the show about a family just like our family. This family had two parents in their mid-forties who lived in the suburbs just as we did. Produced for Screen Gems by Eugene B. Rodney and Robert G. Young, who also played the fa-ther, the show was called *Father Knows Best*.

The Andersons, James C. (called Jim), Margaret, and their three children, seventeen-year-old Betty with her ponytail, fourteen-year-old Bud, and nine-year-old Kathy, lived at 607 South Maple Street in Springfield, Ohio. Betty was called Princess. The Cheevers, Mary and John and their three chil-dren—teenaged, ponytailed Susie, ten-year-old Ben, and baby Fred—lived on Scarborough Station Road in Scarborough, New York. The Andersons were played by the open-faced Robert Young, with a reassuring manner that served him well in his later role of Marcus Welby, M.D., and the slightly ditsy Jane Wyatt, who wore a shirtwaist dress often covered by an apron, pearl stud earrings, and brown hair in the kind of flip that required nightly bobby pins. She looked just like my mother. The Andersons had met at Jackson College, where Margaret's sorority was Iota Theta. My parents had met after my mother graduated from college, Sarah Lawrence, in the office of a literary agent where my mother was a secretary. Jim Anderson wore bow ties; my father wore bow ties.

Every Wednesday night, homework or no homework, I settled expectantly on the gray carpet in front of the magic box as the up-beat introductory music played and the credits began to roll. By the time the screen told me that the show was presented by Scott Paper, I was in television heaven. I loved the exterior shot of the Anderson house. Although I knew it was a stage set on the Columbia Pictures lot in Hollywood, I thought it looked just like our house. I reveled in the familiar smiling faces of each character as their names came on the screen: Jim and Margaret and Betty, or Princess, baseball-loving Bud, and moon-faced Kathy, who was sometimes called Kitten. As the Cheever family dog, named Cassiopeia after an obscure constellation, snuffled around and my mother did the dinner dishes in the kitchen or folded laundry, I gave myself over to the perfectly nicknamed Andersons and their beautifully well-timed lives. I dreamed of being called Princess. The series covered all the normal family crises faced by an American family in the 1950s—Betty's yearning for a formal dress, Bud's love of baseball and his troublesome neighborhood pranks. The Andersons were upset when a new highway was built near their house; my parents were upset when a new highway was built near our house.

On *Father Knows Best*, the siblings squabble and the parents have disagreements, and all this is somehow magically resolved by the end of the half-hour-long show. The show's producer, Eugene

Rodney, said that he liked the writers—including Roswell Rogers and Paul West—to create stories with "built-in moral lessons." Although even Jim Anderson often doesn't know best on his own show, it's his authority that is without question. He can rant and rail about having to go to an office, he can complain about the expense of clothes and sports, but everyone knows that it is his job to provide both financial and emotional security for his family, just as it is his wife's job to provide domestic comfort for them. They live in a world where, as my grandmother used to say, there is a place for everything and everything in its place. In their world, Father knows best. Daughters are princesses. Women are happy in the kitchen and men go unquestioningly to the office. Jim may be a midlevel executive but at home he is a king. My father was a writer, and at home he tried to pretend to be king. The only adult writer on *Father Knows Best* is Harper Emes, Jim's high-school teacher who gave up his job to embrace a career in literature. He has yet to publish a book. He is a failure. In the meantime, Jim lends him money. Emes is just one of the friends who drop into the series, even as my parents' friends from the past were always dropping in on us in Scarborough.

On the surface, my family life was very much like the Andersons'. "Parties on Friday and Saturday, and on Sunday we take a walk," my father wrote in his journal in the winter of 1957. That winter in an episode titled "A Trip to Hillsborough," Bud Anderson and his friend Kippy decided to be writers and take the commuter train down to the next station on the line—Hillsborough—to gather life experience. At the last minute Kippy was busy, so Bud went alone, and when they found out that he was by himself, Jim and Margaret panicked. He was too young to travel alone. Bud was safe, of course. None of *us* ever felt quite safe. My father was a writer who had finally published a novel. "The wind off the river is very cold," he continued in the journal. "But in sheltered places where the sun shines we can smell the earth and, oh, I am very happy with all of this, the valley, my wife, my children and the sky. And then I think of secrets and mysteries, those forms that lie way below our commonest worries."

Father Knows Best didn't think much about secrets and mysteries, and Jim Anderson, the handsome, matter-of-fact father, wasn't given to elegiac responses to nature or examinations of his own feelings. Oh, how I longed for the simpler version of family that I saw on our black-and-white television screen, as my real-life mother bustled around in our tiny kitchen preparing the family dinner, and my Technicolor father sat in the yellow wing chair and swirled the ice in his bourbon, and my little brothers pounded around the house playing boy games. Episodes like the one in which Margaret uses "the female art of persuasion" to get Jim to take dancing lessons, or the one in which she finally gets the coveted object that was every woman's dream—a mink coat—gave me something to aspire to: a conventional, normal, happy version of the fractured life I seemed to be living. In this life, I would be called Princess. Instead, my parents often fought. My mother liked to tell us that we had exactly ten dollars left in the bank; my father was fond of predicting that we would lose our rented house and have nowhere to live. My father was sarcastic, and my mother sometimes left the dinner table in tears. My father would stonily serve the rest of the dinner she had cooked, usually ham with pineapple, or creamed chipped beef with two accompanying vegetables cooked within an inch of their lives.

At school in those days we lived in fear, our fear of teachers and grades dwarfed by the fear of World War III or the H-bomb or the missiles that we daily expected Cold War hostilities would send from the dreaded Communists. The Communists were evil. Friends had moved away because they said that living near the Hudson River as we did meant we would be vulnerable to the radioactive cloud as it moved up from the city after the bomb dropped. Other neighbors were building bomb shelters. We heard that some had guns to keep us out because they didn't have enough in their underground bunkers to share. On a clear night in the Hudson Valley my father would take us outside to see if we could get a glimpse of *Sputnik,* the space satellite the Russians had launched that year. They had beaten us in space. Here on earth it seemed to be just a matter of time. My parents read Nevil Shute's terrifying *On the Beach* about the end of the world. The Andersons had bookcases just as we did—in fact, their living room, with its central couch and large, curtained window, could have been a replica of ours—but they didn't read the kind of book that scared the life out of you.

Watching an old tape of *Father Knows Best,* I am amazed by how contrived it seems. You can tell that the actors are reading lines. Everyone speaks perfect English in slightly affected accents, even Princess. There is no slang. In one episode, Jim decides to teach his children how lucky they are to live in America by giving them a taste of twenty-four hours in "tyrant land." Although it is never mentioned, this is clearly an episode about the threat of Communism. Jim issues his children numbers and assigns them jobs. He explains that in "tyrant land" there are no personal possessions. They're horrified, and their anguish is increased when it turns out that Bud can't go out for his baseball game and Betty can't go on a hayride with Ralph because their "tyrant" father won't let them. In the end, the children come to appreciate the freedom they have as Americans and Jim and Margaret come to appreciate how hard it is to behave as tyrants.

Compared to today's families, with their fragmented power lines and scattered chains of command, families in which both parents work and no one really knows whose job it is to put dinner on the table, the Anderson family looks like a small, pleasant island in some archipelago of nostalgia. No wonder it was a huge hit, winning six Emmys in the years between 1954 and 1963 and being shown for years after production had stopped. Even now it has legions of fans, people who have the time to argue about whether there were 203 or 206 episodes, or who have downloaded the upbeat introductory tune onto their websites.

A lot has happened in the past fortysomething years. Some things stay the same, though. At least one night a week, homework or no homework, my children and I cluster around the color television with its one thousand channels to watch our favorite sitcom about an all-American family with three children who also live in Springfield, USA. Our favorite family, who are as much America's favorites as the Andersons were, are the Simpsons. My father was more Homer than James Anderson, anyway. He had Homer's drinking habits, and Homer's ambivalence about almost everything. I and my brothers were certainly more Bart than Betty.

The Simpsons represent the worst of the American family. They have serious problems that will never go away. The Andersons represented the best of the American family, living in a world where difficulties were always learning experiences. They were what we wanted to be, I thought then. Yet somehow the Andersons are depressing. The world seemed like a very small place in those days. It was a time when a woman's highest ambition was to be a good housewife, a time when men were judged primarily on their ability to provide financial support and domestic authority, a time when happily ever after was preferable to a real life with all its delights, a time when my own dream of glory was to be a conventional suburban teenager with a tacky nickname. The world seemed limited by the walls of the family ranch house. No one ever told the truth, even on television. The Simpsons, on the other hand, make us laugh at ourselves. They are our worst selves, and we love them for it.

THE GREAT ONES

Barry Hannah

In the early fifties television came to my little town, Clinton, in Mississippi. The green and yellow fields came close to every step you made. Cornfields were not that far from City Hall. We were so used to the train running through, its wail was only a lullaby right before you slept. The tracks separated black from white homes. The streets were brick on the white, south side. Some white homes of slumping prosperity were on the north side, but you soon got into a real shantytown of black folks, where wood fires were always going. The southwest quadrant of our village (pop. 2,500) was a little Baptist college, across the street from a large Baptist church. Lesser churches carried on, too, but were largely mute in the general sway of the Baptists. Even Presbyterians were strange in my town. There was no crime, and children roamed freely.

I could mention the social catastrophe inflicted on the impoverished blacks, now as I write, but I grew up in Clinton ignorant of this. Let me venture an accurate estimate of my place in the fifties: It was nonviolent apartheid. When I was about fifteen, a carload of buddies and I made our third trip to cherry-bomb the Black Cat nightclub in Shantytown when we heard an extra explosion behind us. A fed-up black man had shotgunned the back end of my Chevy Belair. This woke my soul to my own cruelty and to the fact that blacks might be human like me. You would not want a cherry bomb in your dancing quarters. Still, I could not get over the gall of this creature with a lethal weapon. I could not fully conceive of this response.

I give such attention to time and place so as to illuminate the entrance of television. Before beer, before cigarettes. And I confess with no shame that Froggy the Gremlin on *The Smiling Ed McDonald Show*, Ernie Kovacs, Sid Caesar, and Jonathan Winters shaped whoever I am gravely, gravely. For a good while television was bad. Old Hopalong Cassidy movies, and a "test pattern"—does anyone remember this early curiosity?—that came on at, say, ten P.M. when the station had nothing else to show for the day. For some reason the center of this pattern was the head of an Indian chief emanating rays like drawn radar. Many to whom I write now will confess, with me, that we *watched* the test pattern to see if it would do anything. This was not the height of boredom but rather a kind of pathetic worship of the Indian void. Even still life on the tube promised another world.

My father was late in getting us television. Dad was making his way in the world. We were soon to move from our abode into the requisite abode of prosperity in the Eisenhower years, the ranch-style house, and Dad was tight, against the frivolous. But I needed television so deeply, I would sit in a neighbor's yard in a lawn chair, watching what I could of their television through a pair of binoculars. I would wangle invitations from odd new friends who had TV. Then we at last owned our own blond-cabineted Sylvania.

Our Miss Brooks, The Ed Sullivan Show, The Jackie Gleason

Show—these were good enough shows, and I did see Elvis with his pelvic moves censored. By then the preachers were wailing and on the attack against the new jungle music. It seems the preachers were wailing and railing during most of my youth.

But I largely ignored Elvis and fell for a show that was a bit young for me, *Smiling Ed McDonald.* I recall a horde of kids in a great auditorium. These children could really scream with delight, and best, they, like me, waited eagerly for the appearance of Froggy the Gremlin. "Plunk your magic twanger, Froggy!" somebody would say, and out came this croaking puppet. The place went wild. I don't remember what Froggy did besides his main act. Some opera singer, fat, or a lecturer in the arts would take the stage to give a sincere, affected speech about music or art or the sunrise when suddenly, behind them, Froggy the Gremlin would burst in with a squawked word entirely destructive to the solemnity of the lecturer. The lecturer would repeat the word that Froggy had said, again and again. Eventually the lecturer would collapse and dive offstage while the kids, again, roared. They loved the humiliation. Perhaps they were watching their teachers. "To train for the opera, one must first have—" Comes in Froggy: "Big rubber boots!" "Yes, one must have big rubber boots. No, no!" Froggy would be in the background jumping around with glee. Now as I write I would say, with the words I didn't own then, that Froggy was the destruction of pretentiousness, affectedness, or sententiousness. After Froggy, I've always been on the watch for those qualities throughout my listening to "pros" or reading anybody. Froggy lurks. I find "Big rubber boots!" in a big croak erupting from me in my own work also. And I thrive on the collapse and humiliation of the sententious everywhere. In fact I look forward to it. Do Froggy and I.

I was ready for Camus and his book *The Fall,* I think, wherein the protagonist hears mysterious laughter behind him. He turns and there's nobody there. He is a judge. Froggy connects, always, and keeps you straight. I remember and appropriate a line from Ferlinghetti here about the poet's "constantly risking absurdity . . . and death." Oh yes. And Froggy close behind.

Let nobody puffy get away with it. Lord God, there have been a herd of the puffy in poetry readings I've been forced to attend. More of us should blurt and croak throughout these excruciations. Enough of this automatic Episcopal reverence and the required clapping of hands at the end, no matter how puny the reading. Big rubber boots! Yet one must practice pity and phony reverence *all the way* through adulthood.

Many have forgotten, or have never known, how fine black-and-white television was. We made our own fun (and our own destruction) in my town and we did not stop when television came. There are many hollows in black-and-white television (and, of course, movies) in which to imagine. Your mind is happy filling those hollows. With color, which I, of course, thought was another joyful revolution, there is total plentitude. Your mind is stopped by the fullness, the dead-on illuminated accuracy. But in early television, much of it shot on a soundstage, your head and even body could get in. You played along with the television people. You could bring your whole town with you, your friends. It was a ball to watch a show with your pals. We knew TV was a miraculous invention, magic, in fact. We were such participants, wholesale, and such hicks, we didn't dare to know *how* it worked. Leave magic alone, please. I would have been annoyed to hear about this instrument reduced to physics, particle waves. Please. It just *was,* like an airplane. Nowadays I miss the wonder and awe we had as small-town yard brats. Shut up, back there in the laboratory. Big rubber boots! And we did not so much watch the set; we *clung* to it. Nobody went around back of the set to see how they got the little people in there—not even us hicks. But if we had seen the little people back there, we would have forced our way in to join them.

A bit later came Sid Caesar. My memory is curious and very spotty about Caesar and company. I recall Caesar sweating, cross-eyed, sputtering. He simply was a damned fool over and over again, in any role—a pirate, a businessman, an emperor in the East with a way big-assed sword. He was just not getting the hang of it. His costar Imogene Coca was perfect, drab and scrawny and simply overcome. The pair would now remind me of derelicts in a Samuel Beckett play. The black and white of that show seemed so grainy and raw, Caesar and Coca appeared to be wrestling with the medium itself. But I am getting a bit French and smarty-pantish here. Big rubber boots. The sweat, the panting, the mis-comprehension of everything, the clown so hard-put in a gray flannel suit—this was Caesar. I took him into my bosom. The beauty of being a lad around early TV is that you had no idea thousands, then millions of other Americans were sharing Caesar and other delights with you. You were confident these wonderful creatures were yours alone.

Then comes the divine Jonathan Winters. A friend of mine once told me he got in stitches *before* Winters ever said a word. Winters, the genius of voices. Especially the Ohio rube who com-prehends just enough to deform any given event. I remember best the report of the farmer who witnesses the hippies at Woodstock. As with much great art, especially comedy, to attempt to analyze the voice, the mode, the delivery of Winters is to sin against him. He was a man of voices and mouth noises and a very real narra-tor. The mouth noises—for instance, popping a dried cat carcass off the highway and sailing him over the cornfield. "And brother, that's a sailcat," ends Winters, after a long story about what a sail-cat is. The great pops against the side of his head he could per-form, or an arrow coming into you with a sucking sound, were showstoppers on their own. Whereas Caesar and Ernie Kovacs, the last character I would like to eulogize, were very urban, Winters came from Middle America, with its oral narrations, and my friends and I felt included. He sounded like the yokels right in town telling their own benighted yarns. They could be the deacons of the church or the football coach or the high-school principal. More and more we were hip to other lives, and especially other hysterias. Winters could work the microphone—those sounds, those sounds—better than anybody around. I practiced and performed them all through the halls of school and out in the fields. Machine-gun fire, arrows sucking the wind before they hit you. Ricochets—Lord, yes, I could do them. I stole from Winters and got a reputation. Once, while working for Robert Altman, the director, I attended a party at his home in Malibu. He was friends with Winters, and I waited for him. There were other stars—Jim Garner, Ray Walston, Henry Gibson—but no Winters yet. I was trembling, trembling over Winters's advent. I wasn't sure I could stand it if he *did* appear. I was thirty-nine years old. He never showed. What would I have said? Would I have fallen on my knees before him?

Ernie Kovacs and his babe of a wife, Edie Adams, count deeply to me in many ways. Last, first. I was encouraged to know a comic could marry such a woman. So later I myself married high-fetching babes in great confidence. Kovacs was surreal. Most of all I loved Percy Dovetonsils, a lisping poet in a quilted sateen jacket, and with perhaps a quill. He wore spectacles of incredible thickness. The eyes behind them seemed tiny and spiraling. He would unlimber one poem after another out of this pained myopia, and in that lisp. You knew he hadn't a clue, and it was altogether sweet and altogether hysterical, although Kovacs's poet was quiet and reverent. Like many, I learned to make fun of poetry long before I ever saw any real poetry. Later I was to try my hand at "verse" and get bragged on by the English teacher, Mrs. Black-well. But I was always conscious of Percy Dovetonsils, and it was a great victory when my poems sounded nothing like Percy's.

The other high absurdity of Kovacs's that I most recall was the Nairobi Trio, three performers in ape suits playing a sort of retarded chamber music. They wore derbies, were quite serious about their work, and carried on soberly. Great absurdity and great surrealism evoke the deep question Why? Why? in the viewer/listener. There is no earthly reason to have apes doing this. Kovacs answered the call time and again. I think nowadays we are so boiled in constant absurdity (vide MTV), we've lost the ability to respond to it. A geezer comment, but I'm confident it's true.

My friends and I stole this skit outright and then defaced it by our own uses. We were on TV with it—*Teen Tempos*. We had a drummer, a viola player, and a pianist. We were not apes, just sensitive musicians, on the order of Percy Dovetonsils. The skit was: All of us played until the violist made a mistake. I, the drummer, shot him with a blank pistol and he, a large boy, collapsed and really writhed around. The pianist and I began again until the pianist made a mistake, whereupon I shot him. He was a little thin dude but with the spectacles of Dovetonsils. He died calmly, just a bump on the keyboard. Then I, the drummer, continued alone. Not the faintest hint of remorse or lonesomeness on my face. Ain't that funny? C'mon, c'mon, ain't it? We had wide fame locally and played the anniversary show.

It is sufficient to conclude here that these comics and a puppet, Froggy, were in my blood, and are still. I have fumbled a bit with the chronology here, but I don't care, and you don't. Winters made appearances on many shows, and had his own show briefly. Not surprisingly, it failed—Winters should be a short story, not seen too regularly—although pieces of it are still acts of genius. Caesar, Froggy, and Kovacs remained in black and white but must be revered for what they did for thousands, and especially for yokels with some wit like me, next to green and yellow fields, brick streets, and vast and deep censure by the Baptist Church, deacons, but much more fiercely, religious mothers in league with the pastor and those sour theologians on the college campus. What freedom these television souls put in your head, your blood-stream.

May I explain throwing cherry bombs into a black club? What were we thinking? Were we thinking television? No. We *were* television, the avant garde of television. The black fellow shot the end of my car with scattershot and I've not harmed a black person since, in any fashion. I learned my lesson.

My friends and I were an after-school special, don't you see? We were out there on the winds of danger when all the others were sitting at home watching television, the Wasteland, as it became.

THE ANDY GRIFFITH SHOW

Jill McCorkle

I was two years old when *The Andy Griffith Show* premiered in 1960. It aired on CBS, Mondays at 9:30 P.M. This is a great time slot for a sitcom but not for a kid. Occasionally, during the last season (1968), I got to stay up, but by then the show was nothing like what I had been watching late afternoons for the past several years. My sister and I faithfully had a whole series of shows we watched while waiting for the changing of the guard—that is, when our mother, who got off work at five, arrived home and Louise Caple, our baby-sitter, left. By five o'clock Louise had already had us bathe and put on pajamas and eat something good and starchy—grits, macaroni and cheese—so we were slightly drugged on carbs and quietly glued to the television when our parents settled us in for the night. We watched *The Huckleberry Hound Show* and *The Flintstones*, and we watched *The Andy Griffith Show*. Opie was little, Barney was front and center, and Helen Crump—the schoolteacher who ends the series as the love interest who will become Mrs. Andy Taylor—had not yet moved to Mayberry.

In other words, I was, as a ten-year-old, already clinging to the past. Those rare times when I maneuvered my way into late-night TV, I was struck by the harshness of color. Don't ask how this struck me, seeing as how we didn't have a color TV, but I had heard about it and somehow had been greatly influenced.

A lot of people might say that this influence was the result of parental suggestion that color looked cheap and garish. We knew people who had spent a lot of money and now watched people with green faces. There were a lot of people resisting the move to color for sure. But this wasn't it. The town of Mayberry just didn't fare as well with color. Or maybe it was that Opie (Ron Howard) was no longer the adorable little redheaded boy with the big heart (in one episode he saves up money to buy his girlfriend a new coat) or who runs away from home for fear that his pa is disappointed in him. I loved Opie. He was just right for me. But the shock of seeing him as an adolescent in a rock band saying "Groovy" and "Daddyo" just didn't do it for me. Where was my Opie? Fortunately, he resurfaced (post awkward adolescence) as Richie Cunningham in *Happy Days* and I could once again claim him as the perfect All-American Boy. But it wasn't just the color that I knew was there, or the pubescence of Opie. It was the absence of Don Knotts, in my opinion, one of the greatest comedic actors of all time. I type this actually while staring at an autographed photo of Don Knotts as Barney Fife that my husband gave me for Christmas last year—a treasure.

There is a wonderful website that should be of great interest to all television addicts: www.jumptheshark.com. "Jumping the Shark" refers to an episode of *Happy Days* when the Fonz is water-skiing in his leather jacket in shark-infested waters. It was the moment when many viewers determined that the show had taken a downward turn. Opie/Richie had moved on to become the extremely successful movie director he is today (it was always obvious that Opie Taylor would grow up into a fine man who would do great things!), and the show would never be the same.

Now the term is used to describe any show that has passed its prime, but the majority vote on *The Andy Griffith Show* is that the show jumped when Don Knotts left. I felt it like a death, and even though I tried to give Warren every chance (Jack Burns of the comic team Burns and Schreiber), and to annoy each other my sister and I mimicked his obnoxious manner of repeating and finishing everyone's sentences, he could not replace the huge void left by Barney. The last two years marked a slow and sad decline into *Mayberry RFD*, where Andy was rarely sighted, and viewers like me clung to the hope that one day a Greyhound bus would arrive at the Mayberry station and there would be good ole Barn, sporting his famous salt-and-pepper suit and filled with stories about what was happening in the capital city of Raleigh. He'd pick up some cashew-nut fudge and head on over to Thelma Lou's; the two would get married and all would be right in the world again.

And perhaps this very nostalgia that fills me whenever I think about the series is in fact a product of the true genius behind what evolved. The series began with Andy Griffith leaning more toward his funny hick *No Time for Sergeants* role and Barney as the epitome of a bumbling idiot. However, they eased into their characters, and in no time, Andy was the straight man, and though Barney remained the butt of most of the jokes, we glimpsed his vulnerable side often enough that he was a real person—a person we loved and genuinely cared about. There were those tender episodes, usually involving a rendition of the Mayberry Union High alma mater and Andy and Barney reminiscing, or a scene (as many shows ended) out on the front porch with Andy strumming his guitar. These were the episodes that ultimately stole my heart. I recognized myself in both Andy and Barney. We all aspire to Andy's sound wisdom and quick wit—he is the perfect father, friend, husband, citizen. And yet we feel all too close to Barney's inadequacies and recognize the desire to try too hard, to come in second or third place or even last. Once you get to know Barney, you know there's a lot more to this boy (who gave his parents a septic tank for an anniversary present) than meets the eye. These quieter episodes I also easily associated with my own life.

The writer Barry Hannah has said that Southern children are nostalgic by the age of nine or ten, and he is absolutely right. I watched those reruns faithfully, and found myself mourning the loss of Mayberry, or really the loss of my hometown, Lumberton, where my parents had grown up before me. It was their town I mourned. Their town *was* Mayberry, and when I went to visit my grandmother—away from the new neighborhoods with ranch-style houses and split-levels, and away from I-95, which had recently sliced through our town—I could see it all again: the sidewalks my parents had walked as children, the huge elms and pecan trees, the Carolina and Riverside theaters. Instead of Walker's Drugstore, where Andy's first love interest (played by Elinor Donahue, who was Betty on *Father Knows Best* and, most recently, Chris Elliott's mother on *Get a Life*) worked, we had Hegpeth's Pharmacy. It still existed in my childhood and looked just like Walker's, with the old Formica booths and heavy spinning bar stools. My grandfather had been a barber, and though he died before I was born, in my mind, his shop looked just like Floyd's and I imagined long, slow afternoons—fans whirring and people talking while he snipped hair and shaved the faces of prominent men in town. Myer's Lake could have been White Lake or a part of the Lumber River where there once had been a skating rink and rides. In my grandmother's world, and that of my parents' childhood, sitting on the porch was still a form of entertainment, as was walking to the store for ice cream or a soda. Barney has said on numerous occasions: You know what I think I'll do? Think I might go down to Wally's station. Get a bottle of pop. [Rock and doze] Yep, you know what I think I'll do?

My best friend from high school and college roommate, whom I still speak with many times a week, and I have to be careful when in a group that we don't slip into speaking Andy Griffith shorthand. There are so many wonderful quotable lines, especially Barney's many malaprops and mispronunciations, that to avid fans it is indeed a language of sorts. Things like, "Have you got a hand-washing compellshun?" or "He's real swave, all right," or "Dr. Frood would say that is very therapetic."

To say that I have seen all the episodes is an understatement. I have seen them all numerous times. If the show is on (except the ones in color—I am a snob, I'll admit), I have to watch it. Not to would be like turning off a home movie, for within all those reruns I see every inch of my life and all that I know of my parents' lives when they were growing up. It's like a visit. Sometimes I just have it on to hear the voices and the classic lines: "Now, don't get your skinny little veins to poppin'" or "You beat all, you know that?" (Andy to Barney) or Goober's (George Lindsey's) impersonation of Cary Grant ("Judy, Judy, Judy") or one of my favorite sideline characters, Ernest T. Bass, the crazy mountain man who came whooping and hollering down from the mountains to claim a woman to be his bride. "You ain't heard the last of Ernest T. Bass," he yells, followed by maniacal laughter. (His appearances usually coincide with those of Denver Pyle as Briscoe Darling, his daughter, Charlene, and the boys—a somber-faced bunch who could play the hell out of some banjos.) Or Barney trying to sing: "Nita . . . Juuaaaanita . . ." (Juanita, the waitress, along with Sarah, the telephone operator, are two prominent presences who remain offstage.) Or the crystal-clear, beautiful voice of Rafe Hollister singing "Lonesome Road." Charlene Darling is famous for saying, "Don't sing that one, Pa. It makes me cry." I cannot count the times that I have been embarrassed to have my family find me sitting there crying over *The Andy Griffith Show,* or, equally as bad, in complete hysterics over something that I know by heart. Among my favorite episodes (and there are far too many to count) I still rank "Two Fun Girls," where Barney (to Andy's horror) brings Daphne and Skippy—alcohol-swilling bleached-blond bimbos—to the courthouse, which sets off a night of mishaps and blow-ups, and "Barney's First Car," where Barney is duped into buying a lemon from a Ma Barker type who is posing as a sweet little widow lady.

Having grown up feeling like television was one of my dearest friends, I find there are many of those early sitcoms that take me back. Just hearing the theme songs will often make me homesick. I hear the music to *All in the Family* or *The Mary Tyler Moore Show* and something clicks in my brain and I am thinking it should be Saturday night and my dad should be alive and out in the yard with the dwindling coals where he had earlier grilled T-bones. My hair should smell like Prell and I should be feeling slightly depressed that I have to go to Sunday school in the morning, and a little shamed that I've chosen the Saturday-night lineup of Archie and Mary and Bob Newhart and Carol Burnett over any and all friends. There was nothing I loved more except perhaps my dog, who was right there with me finishing off the steak bones. I loved Dick Van Dyke with a passion and had since I was about five. I could quote lengthy scenes from *I Love Lucy* and tried to imitate her wonderful faces and physical movements. I wanted to be in a show at the Tropicana. I wanted to look like That Girl and date Donald Hollinger. I wanted Brian Keith to be my uncle. But where were they, these people I adored? They were in Manhattan and Queens and Chicago and Minneapolis, places I had only glimpsed on the map.

But Mayberry. Mayberry was my town. I knew where Mt. Airy was. I had been to Raleigh and in my college years even made a pilgrimage over to Siler City, where it was rumored that Frances Bavier, who played Aunt Bee, was nutty and lived with hundreds of cats. I didn't push that investigation or the ones where I heard that there were tensions on the set with Aunt Bee. I preferred the wonderful statements by people like Opie—all grown up and having done everyone proud—that Andy Griffith and Don Knotts were wonderful. Stop. That's all I need to know. In my mind, as well as in TV land, Mayberry is forever spinning. It's a slow life, a peaceful life, a good Southern life. Sometimes I like to imagine that Barney and Thelma Lou got married and at this very minute are splitting their pan of cashew fudge and thinking about catching that new Cary Grant movie except they know that Gomer and Goober are already there and will talk too much. The Darlings have put down their banjos for the night. Ernest T. has found himself a girl "what loves him." Aunt Bee has washed all the dishes and is indoors chatting on the phone with her best friend, Clara Edwards. Opie is all tucked in bed with nothing on his mind other than the fishing trip he and his pa will get up and go on in the morning. And Andy is out on the front porch smoking a cigarette because the state crop couldn't hurt you back then, and as far as you can hear, there's quiet. This is Mayberry, North Carolina, and within these city limits the world will always be a good, safe place. As it's been for more than forty years.

"BEAM ME UP, SCOTTY"

James Alan McPherson

Until the terrible terrorist attacks in New York, I had lost contact with television. Beyond the evening news and an occasional episode of *Frasier,* I gave up on the outlet that had once claimed so much of my attention. The reason? It seemed to me that as communications technology became more and more sophisticated, the human dimensions of the shows became more and more banal.

The suspicions I harbored were first confirmed, for me at least, by the cultural critic Morris Berman in his insightful *The Twilight of American Culture.* In this meditation Berman observed that "We live in a collective adrenaline rush, a world of endless promotional/commercial bullshit that marks a deep systemic emptiness, the spiritual equivalent of asthma." Moreover, Berman observed that "vital Kitsch, the promotion of commercial energy at the expense of genuine contact, of real substance, will be the reality for most Americans in the twenty-first century, in one form or another, and it will be fueled by the globalization process."

Morris Berman seems to have been on the mark. The introduction of "reality TV," for example, besides trashing traditional notions of privacy, actually seems to celebrate analogies to the arenas of ancient Rome during its decadence, a period during which a focus on entertainment, however bizarre, served as a palliative for the appetites of the mob. Critics have located the origins of "reality TV" in some of the popular game shows of the 1960s (*The Gong Show, The Dating Game, The Newlywed Game*) pioneered by Chuck Barris. Now, it seems, shows like *Meet My Folks, American Idol,* and *The Bachelor* have inspired the networks, not to mention their commercial sponsors, to rethink the place of scripted series by Hollywood studios. This move would sound a death knell for writers who depend on the studios for employment. And a growing number of critics believe that it would also sound the death knell for good taste.

Morris Berman is one of these critics. But instead of trying to fight or reverse these developments, he cautions, one should simply accept them as a given of contemporary American culture and consider, instead, what he terms the "monastic option":

> *Individual shifts in life ways and values may just possibly act as a wedge that would serve as a counterweight to the world of schlock, ignorance, social inequality, and mass consumerism that now deforms the landscape. At the very least, these "new monks," or native expatriates, as one might call them, could provide a kind of record of authentic ways of living that could be preserved and handed down, to resurface later on, during a healthier time.*

Berman finds a precedent for this "monastic option" in *Fahrenheit 451,* a work of science fiction by Ray Bradbury, that had emerged from American popular culture. In this novel, in a futuristic society, the reading of books is a crime. But a group of dedicated readers go "underground" in order to memorize, and thus preserve, the great books. Fahrenheit 451 is the exact temperature at which paper ignites.

By exploring Morris Berman's "monastic option," it is still possible to locate, if one wanders away from the conventional pathways, havens of vitality. For example, as the introduction of the DVD format has begun to displace the VHS format in movies, video stores began to sell their stocks of VHS tapes. No sense of aesthetic taste ruled these decisions to sell: Great classics became available at the same price as the purely popular movies.

In a video store in Cedar Rapids, Iowa, I found a particular treasure. This movie chain outlet was, true to the trend, continuing its transition to the DVD format by selling old VHS tapes. The cost was $2.99 per tape, and you got two free tapes for every two purchased. Among the many VHS tapes was a full shelf of the original *Star Trek* episodes. I purchased the entire shelf. I had always liked this series, from its inception in late 1966 to its end in 1969. I always made time to watch it. There was something captured in the original series that began to fade out of its later reincarnations. Watching the episodes that I had seen many years before, I recognized in them elements drawn from the Western movie genre. Space, to Gene Roddenberry, the creator of *Star Trek*, was indeed "the final frontier." And like the Western, it provided a stage, a backdrop, against which essentially human situations could be dramatized. And both stages, I learned, had their origins in another expression of the American vernacular: the dime novel.

One of the most vital expressions of American popular culture, this innovation had its beginnings during and after the Civil War, when a new technology allowed the use of wood chips, rather than more expensive cloth, to provide disposable paper. The American News Company pioneered the use of pulp to print newspapers that would keep the nation, or at least the North, up to date about the events of that war. But soon ambitious businessmen began to use pulp to print the dime novels. So an industry was started, one that began to project popular heroes. Soon a group of pulp novelists—Ned Buntline, Owen Wister, Lou Senaris, Zane Grey—began to place their heroes on the Western "stage," where they straddle two radically different worlds. There is the in-group, one that is more civilized, and an out-group, one that is much more fierce and adaptable, more skilled in matters of survival. The hero is a synthesis of these two sets of characteristics. Like J. Fenimore Cooper's Leatherstocking, the hero mediates between the two, almost always on behalf of the in-group. After he succeeds, he has one of two choices: Either he joins the in-group and conforms to its mores, or else he rides away.

But the American pulp novel also pioneered the beginnings of a uniquely American take on science fiction. Although it is conventional to locate the beginnings of this genre in the writings of Mary Shelley and H. G. Wells, its American strain emerged during the 1860s, at a time when the demands of the Civil War caused extreme innovations in American technology. In Edward S. Ellis's *The Huge Hunter* (1868), a young man named Frank Reed, from Brooklyn, together with his cousin, visiting from Missouri, build a black steam man with Negro features and wearing a top hat. They drive him out to the prairies and employ him in hunting Indians and saving the lives of settlers. Edgar Rice Burroughs's Tarzan series grew out of this very same tradition. It was not until later, probably beginning with the dime novels of Zane Grey, that the Western and the technology-based science fiction genre were separated, one located in the Western landscape, the other in space. These two "stages" operated independently of each other, the frontier stage in a great number of classic Westerns, the space stage in everything from Georges Méliè's *Voyage to the Moon* (1902) to *Harry Potter and the Sorcerer's Stone* (2001).

It was not until *Star Trek* premiered on television on September 8, 1966, that the stages were re-integrated. Gene Roddenberry, the creator of the series, had worked first as a writer for the television series *Have Gun Will Travel*, with a Western hero named Paladin. Roddenberry thus brought to his new creation, *Star Trek,* an intimate understanding of the conventions of the Western. His ambition for the new series, he recalled in a later interview, was "an attempt to say that humanity will reach maturity and wisdom on the day that it begins, not just to tolerate, but to take a special delight in, differences in ideas and differences in life forms. We tried to say that the worst possible thing that can happen to all of us is for the future to somehow press us into a common mold where we begin to act and talk and look alike. If we cannot learn to actually enjoy these small differences between our kind here on this planet, then we do not deserve to go out into space and meet the diversity that is almost certainly out there."

One hears in this statement an echo of the idealism of the 1960s. John Glenn had pioneered space flight in 1962, almost four years before *Star Trek* premiered. There seemed to have existed at that time an idealistic belief in technology, and thus in space flights (Neil Armstrong's famous "One giant step for mankind") as an instrument for helping us resolve many of our *human* differences and difficulties. This required, however, a balance between the sophisticated technology and the human dimensions of the characters involved in the space adventures. Such was the genius of Roddenberry's contribution. Now, well over thirty years later, it seems that the old balance has been broken and that the technological artifacts have taken on a life of their own, one that has subordinated the once-essential human dimensions of the enterprise. As a matter of fact, in the aftermath of the *Columbia* tragedy, one commentator observed that the terror attacks of September 11, the collapse of the Internet stock boom, and the shuttle explosion may have undercut the technological bravado that helps drive scientific exploration of all sorts. John Staudenmaier, editor of the *Technology and Culture* quarterly at the University of Detroit-Mercy, told the *New York Times*, "There is a feeling of vulnerability right in the center of where Americans tend to feel most confident, our sophisticated technological systems. For Americans, it's almost like being homeless. It leads to an identity crisis."

Because he was obsessive about the balance between the technological and the human, Gene Roddenberry ensured that members of his *Enterprise* crew remembered who they were.

The son of a Los Angeles policeman (who may have been the model for Captain Kirk), Roddenberry was a pilot in the U.S. Air Force during World War II. He was a devoted reader with great imagination and determination. Nowadays, the word *diversity* is nothing more than a politically charged cliché, but Roddenberry's application of it caused him to cast Nichelle Nichols, a black woman, as Lieutenant Uhura, the communications officer on the bridge of the USS *Enterprise*. This was an extremely radical step in 1966, and so was the first televised interracial kiss, between Captain Kirk and Uhura. DeForest Kelley played "Bones," or Dr. McCoy, the stubborn, sharp-tongued but sentimental caretaker of health aboard the starship. Leonard Nimoy played Second Officer Spock, an alien ("Vulcan") with devil-like pointed ears, who embodied Enlightenment and scientific reason. George Takei, the product of Japanese and Filipino bloodlines, played Sulu, the helmsman and weapons officer. Montgomery Scott, played by the Scottish-accented James Doohan, wrapped his accent around a meticulous engineering of the starship. At some point in the series, when it had become popular and the Russians complained that they were not being represented, Roddenberry added Chekov to the crew, and his Russian-accented English blended into the rich ethnic mixture.

This diverse crew was to meet with every imaginable variation on the theme of "diversity" in its episodes. What holds them together is not so much the dependability and efficiency of the starship and its technological resources, as a recognizable ethical system handed down in such a way as to maintain the moral integrity, the *ethos*, of the communal effort, even under the most threatening of galactic circumstances. The crew, acting as an *oikos*, or household, seeks the *ethos* through the use of reason and free will and human resourcefulness. In a democratic sense, the crew members represent a new kind of *ethnos*, or nation, loyal to the prime directives of a multigalactic *polis*, or state. The beauty of the arrangement, in episode after episode, resides in the attempts made by each member of the crew to remain in conformity with this complex hierarchy of values. It is no accident, I believe, that the voice-over prologing each episode ("These are the voyages of the Starship *Enterprise*. Its five-year mission, to explore the reaches of space . . .") echoes the opening lines of Herodotus's *History*:

> *These are the researches of Herodotus of Halicarnassus, which he publishes in the hope of thereby preserving from decay the remembrance of what men have done, and of preserving the great and wonderful actions of the Greeks and the barbarians from losing their due meed of glory; and withal to put on record what were their grounds of feud. . . .*

The show's famous line, "Beam me up, Scotty," was an evocation of the fact that after each adventure, no matter how dangerous, the old hierarchical order was still in place, no matter what terrible technology had been encountered. The statement evoked the understanding that the old balance between the rituals of technology and the rituals of myth, which, in fact derive from the same human sources, were intact.

As I have said, the two defining dimensions of the series—human feelings and technology—were almost always in balance. One of the earliest episodes, "The Enemy Within" (October 6, 1966), explores the results of a disruption of this balance. A transformer malfunction causes Captain Kirk to morph into two radically different selves. One self is savage; the other is overly compassionate and weak. The teaching of the episode is that *both* selves are essential for real leadership, so the two Captain Kirks must be re-integrated, again by computer transport. In another episode, "Who Weeps for Adonis?" members of the crew encounter, on a distant planet, the Greek god Apollo. He has been waiting these many centuries for his "children" to return and resume serving their old gods. But what he encounters are free and independent creatures who no longer need a god to worship or to serve. Reason and technology have freed them from any dependence on supernatural protection. And yet, after a disillusioned Apollo departs to rejoin the other gods, who have long since returned to their distant ancestral home, Kirk reflects on the poignancy of the experience and wonders what it would have been like to have had gods as protectors. "Would it have been such a bad thing?" he asks.

The longest of the episodes, which was the first one in the series submitted by Roddenberry to NBC, is almost epic in its ambitions. Over four episodes, Roddenberry explores what results when the old hierarchical order (*ethos*, *oikos*, *ethnos*, *polis*) is disrupted. At this point, the captain of the *Enterprise* is Christopher Pike, played by Jeffrey Hunter. Spock is Pike's science officer.

Captain Pike is lured into a trap by aliens on Talos IV when he responds to a distress signal from the crew of another ship on the unknown planet. The ship had disappeared eighteen years before, and the crew members whom Pike seeks to rescue prove to be illusions created by their highly intelligent, but nonhuman, alien captors on Talos IV. These captors practice a form of rational decadence. Indeed, they seem to have pioneered their own version of "reality television." They imprison Captain Pike in a cage, explore his memories and his thoughts, and provide him with dramatizations of any fantasies that come into his mind. Their ultimate goal is to mate him with an earth-woman, a woman who was, as a child, a survivor of the wreck of the spaceship on Talos IV. She has been cared for by the aliens, in anticipation of the time when other humans would arrive and the aliens could choose a mate for her. The offspring of this mating, they believe, will allow them to repopulate their dead planet. But Captain Pike rebels against this rationalized plan for his life. He discovers that human *anger* is the one weapon left to him, so he employs it until the aliens see it cannot be easily managed. Captain Pike is allowed to resume his place on the *Enterprise,* and he does so, especially after he sees that the very beautiful woman who was to be his mate is also an illusion. She had been badly scarred in the wreck of her spaceship eighteen years before, and now Captain Pike sees her as she is: old, deformed, a wreckage of a human being. Entitled "The Cage," this was, as I say, the pilot submitted to NBC, and it was not well received, perhaps because it was already a time when studios were interested in happily-ever-after endings.

However, in the two subsequent episodes, after Captain Pike has become, because of an accident, an invalid confined to a wheelchair and Kirk is now captain, Spock breaks the rules of both Starfleet Command (the *polis*) and the *Enterprise* community (the *oikos*) by hijacking the spaceship and taking it back to

Talos IV. Captain Pike is aboard, unable to speak except through technological signals. It is Spock's plan to reunite Captain Pike with the woman he left behind on Talos IV. He achieves this but is court-martialed for breaking with the settled order. Out of loyalty to his friend, Kirk defends Spock. In the process, the viewer is allowed to see the events that had occurred in "The Cage." This episode, partly written by Ray Bradbury, contains both black-and-white and color footage as it recollects the reasons for Spock's rebellious gesture. Gradually, something deeply human comes into focus—an affirmation of the *oikos* that has grown up among Captain Pike, Captain Kirk, and Mr. Spock. Back on the planet, a magical thing happens. Christopher Pike, like the woman, has his health and his youth restored by the aliens. He is allowed to bond with the now-beautiful woman. As Kirk is leaving, the aliens tell him, "Captain Pike now has his fantasy, while you have only reality. We shall see which is the better choice."

This episode deservedly received the Hugo Award, the highest honor for writers of science fiction.

Another episode, "Space Seed" (February 16, 1967), could very easily be an early projection of the media's fascination with Osama bin Laden and Saddam Hussein. It introduces a character named Khan Noonian Singh, who is, curiously, of enhanced genetic origins from the "mysterious Orient"—in this case India. There have been many stock villains in the *Star Trek* episodes— the Romulans, the Klingons—but none is more fascinating than Khan. He is a Shik, one of many genetically improved "supermen" created by earth scientists in the 1990s. This super-race of Caesars, Napoleons, and Alexanders, bred for their leadership abilities, lead an uprising, which is suppressed, and the remnants of the "race" are put aboard "slow ships" and set adrift in space. Two centuries later, the *Enterprise* crew discovers one of the ships, the USS *Botany Bay,* and finds Khan and seventy of his old crew still alive. Once revived by the ship's medical technology, Khan reverts to his old self. He regrets that, centuries before, the earth people failed to appreciate the nobility of his attempt to unify the world under one leader. *"We offered them order!"* he declares. He then lays plots to take over the *Enterprise* and its advanced technology in order to achieve his long-delayed goal. He revives his old crew, courts a romantically inclined female member of the crew, and seizes control. Here begins a great test of wills between Captain Kirk and Khan. Khan is much more intelligent than Captain Kirk, but he lacks compassion. Either the crew of the *Enterprise* will join him, Khan orders, or they will all die. But here, once again, the deeply human dimensions of the crew are dramatized. When Spock denounces Khan, Captain Kirk responds, "We humans have a streak of barbarian in us." And once the crew reclaims the ship from Khan's people, Kirk demonstrates the compassion that is so lacking in Khan. He decides not to kill him. Instead, Khan and his people are to be taken to a distant planet where they can build their own empire. Kirk allows them to cast their genetically superior seeds in space.

This episode dramatizes, once again, the conflict between superior technology and human values, and the viewer is taken back to this very struggle inside Captain Kirk himself in "The Enemy Within." But to underscore the point about the necessity of this uncomfortable alliance between ruthlessness and compassion in human beings, Kirk quotes for Mr. Spock from Milton's *Paradise Lost* in reference to Khan: "It is better to rule in hell than to serve in heaven." Khan was such an appealing character that he later claimed his own full-length movie, *The Wrath of Khan*, in which he returns from his stronghold and tries again to rule the world.

The episodes went on and on and on, examining various segments of the human past on the stage provided by technology: the Roman arena, Chicago gangster life during the 1930s, Adolf

Hitler, the old American West, the hidden emotional undercurrents of Vulcan life when Mr. Spock's genes dictate to him, in a deeply emotional way, that it is time for him to mate. Just as it is said that the American Western movie writers abstracted from ancient Greek dramas (*High Noon*), so the *Star Trek* episodes looked back on, and abstracted from, vital images drawn from human history and popular culture. The show pioneered a uniquely American synthesis of the vernacular and the learned.

But, by this time, the series was having its own trouble with technology. In 1967, relying on its Nielsen ratings, NBC made plans to cancel the show. But *Star Trek* had attracted an audience much too broad and diverse to be gauged by the twelve hundred viewers with Nielsen meters attached to their television sets. Roddenberry expressed his own suspicions about the accuracy of the ratings:

> *One thing ratings, valid or otherwise, have never proven is the loyalty of our series' viewers against another's.* Star Trek, *I discovered, has as devoted a group as any show in history. It is also an intelligent and vocal audience who resent the bland sameness of TV entertainment, and who are fed up with seeing television's one attempt to be different guillotined by a statistical machete. . . .*

Letters of protest began flooding the offices of NBC, 114,667 arriving before the end of 1968, and 52,151 alone the following February. A petition was filed by most of the scientists at the Los Alamos Proving Grounds. One hundred graduate students at Cornell added their voices. Five hundred Cal Tech students joined them, staging a torchlight parade from their campus in Los Angeles to the front door of the NBC studio. Berkeley students

hired a blimp to fly over the city and denounce the television ratings. After more than one million letters arrived, NBC changed
its mind.

In a little town named Riverside, Iowa, less than sixty miles
from Iowa City, during the late 1980s, Gene Roddenberry's vision
came down to earth. A young city council member named Steve
Miller caused a resolution to be passed that created in Riverside
an annual *Star Trek* festival. Why Riverside? In fleshing out the
biography of James T. Kirk, Roddenberry imagined that he had
been born "in a small town in the state of Iowa." But it is proba-
ble that Roddenberry had come to associate Kirk with his collab-
orator, Ray Bradbury, who was born in a small town in Ohio and
who, in his *Martian Chronicles*, took small-town communal values
to the distant planets. Whatever the connection, the communal
values dramatized by Kirk (farm and family, spaceship and crew)
struck a chord in Miller. The Trekfest began in March 1988. Over
the years since then many thousands of fans have attended the
June festival: twenty thousand one year, thirty thousand in others.
They have come from as far away as Japan and Afghanistan. It is
a prototypical small-town festival with dances and demo-derby
events, but with galactic overtones. In appreciation of this event,
Gene Roddenberry gave Steve Miller an award, Honorary Flight
Deck Officer. Riverside, Iowa, now has its own "field of dreams."

Gene Roddenberry once asked: "Can we live in a way that can
manifest spirit in the ever-accumulating life of commerce, technology, and the dazzling new instruments of communication?"
He then went on to explore this issue in an episode, "A Taste of
Armageddon," that aired on February 23, 1967. The *Enterprise*
encounters Eminiar VII, a planet that has been at virtual war with
its neighboring planet, Vendikar, for five hundred years. The war
is fought by computer, and whenever a "hit" is proclaimed by the

computer, a certain number of people report to a disintegration machine. The plot traces the contest between Captain Kirk and the leader of the people of Eminiar VII, who believe religiously that reason and technology should rule. Kirk attempts to stop the virtual war. "No peace!" the leader of the Eminiarians says. "We're a killer species."

"It's instinctive," Captain Kirk agrees, "but the instincts can be fought." And Kirk does stop the war. When questioned by Mr. Spock as they fly away, Kirk discloses that all along he had believed that he could change the virtual reality that had become habitual for the Eminiarians. "You acted on a *feeling*?" Spock asks in amazement. And Captain Kirk replies, "Sometimes a feeling is all that we have to go on."

This was the genius of the original *Star Trek* series. It gave us access to highly sophisticated technology and a dangerous universe. And then it dramatized how human beings much like ourselves, acting on feelings with which we all could identify, resolved conflict after conflict after conflict.

I am very glad now that I have those old tapes, those useful reminders, inside my personal monastery.

BRING BACK BIG VALLEY

Jayne Anne Phillips

> *My valley lies over the ocean*
> *My valley lies over the sea*
> *My valley lies dormant on eBay*
> *Oh, bring back my valley to me*

Some of us remember an American TV landscape replete with cowboys and Westerns. Before psychiatrist-obsessed Mafia dons and cop shows that counted hours, before extraterrestrial conspiracies and reality exhibitionism, cowboys ran the show. On every channel (there were only four) a turn-of-the-century American West held sway. Week after week, men rode their horses out of endless panoramas right into our laps. Stirring theme songs suggested manifest destiny made real. TV dinners were newly invented and terrorism was unthinkable. A man was a man and a woman was Linda Evans as Audra Barkley, blond and blue-eyed, very slightly spunky and protected on all sides by a veritable pantheon of big brothers. Despite her kittenish good looks, Audra was a pale imitation of her mother, Victoria, played by the incomparable Barbara Stanwyck. Stanwyck's Victoria Barkley was the heart of the show, and *The Big Valley* still reigns supreme as the first and only TV Western built around a steely, fifty-plus female character. As Victoria, *Miss* Barbara Stanwyck (as she's respectfully billed in the credits) is, well, fabulous. *The Big Valley* isn't *Stella Dallas, Double Indemnity*, or *Walk on the Wild Side*. Actually, in Stanwyck's film lexicon, *The Big Valley* might stand alongside *The Cattle Queen of Montana*, a vastly less celebrated Stanwyck film. Regardless, Stanwyck emerges unsullied, the (good) single mother of all mothers. She's single by necessity, yes, but very much in charge of her territory *and* her progeny, who (surprise!) love and respect her, seemingly for good reason.

Mothers, take note! Victoria Barkley was nurturing but not clingy, smart but not cold, direct but not didactic, and classy, so classy. No wonder she didn't date! Her dead husband was her only equal on earth and the thought of replacing him never entered her mind—I mean, the minds of the show's writers. Victoria Barkley was a bit like the Virgin Queen: She belonged to her realm and to her subjects, er, her children. *The Big Valley* debuted on September 22, 1965, ran for 112 episodes on ABC, and was canceled by the producer's choice in 1969. A culture had changed and ratings had dropped. Maybe America couldn't watch Victoria Barkley with a straight face anymore: There was so little civility, sanity, and class in our country by 1969 that humming along with the *Big Valley* theme song was simply too painful. Victoria Barkley for president! She would have done a better job.

The Big Valley, in some respects, was not so different from its boys-only counterpart, *Bonanza*. Both shows offered viewers a dynastic choice of favorite sons: Hoss, Adam, or Little Joe, or, in the adjacent valley, *my* valley, Jarrod, Nick, or Heath. Both masculine ensembles provided plenty of story lines resolved in a given time frame and played out against vast Western acreage. All six fraternal heartthrobs had suffered misfortune (the death of a parent) but pulled through to protect the American dream handed down to them. The shows depended not on great acting but on the fact that the characters were always indisputably themselves. Barbara Stanwyck won an Emmy for the show, and no wonder. It was as though Stanwyck, with her superior acting chops, carried the weight for her rather challenged brood and spurred an ever-changing cast of bad guys to greater heights. The show provided paychecks to a long list of young actors, including Harry Dean Stanton, Charles Bronson, Warren Oates, Martin Landau, Ron Howard, Claude Akins, William Shatner, Bruce Dern (twice), and George Kennedy. Jill St. John, Katharine Ross, and Diane Baker were just a few of the girls who passed through as temporary love interests. The sound track played girl music whenever one of them appeared and played it again as they exited town, riding off in stagecoaches, usually, or on trains.

Old West dreams had to do with swagger, and it was mostly men who walked the walk. The men of the Old West were easily contrasted types back in 1965, and *Big Valley* men offered clear choices to housewives cozied up with their black-and-white Philcos after a long day of folding laundry and making Jell-O salads. Bachelor No. 1 was the smart, charming one with the good heart, No. 2 the brash roughneck with the good heart, and No. 3 the wounded outsider with the good heart. The men's men on *The Big Valley* were confirmed singles and dutiful, testosterone-oozing sons whose dating games played out against a backdrop of railroad strikes, range wars, mustang round-ups, earthquakes, land disputes, robberies, kidnappings, and rabid wolves. Little boys wearing fake leather holsters and cradling cap guns could pick a role model to fit their mood. Girl fans, particularly those eleven- and twelve-year-olds juggling dolls and Kotex, never thought twice: They swore their loyalty to Lee Majors's Heath because he *wasn't* yet the Bionic Man. We were on intimate terms with his brothers, too, purely out of devotion to him, but Heath needed us, and we were there for him.

Ah, those Barkleys! For those who never set eyes on the splendor of the valley, let's backtrack. It's 1876. The Barkleys, a truly functional dynasty, oversee their thirty thousand acres in California's San Joaquin Valley (it's a big job: orchards, vineyards, cattle, mines, *and* the property in Mexico). Tom Barkley, the family patriarch, died awhile back—six years back, to be exact—leaving his widow, Victoria, to run the world, er, the ranch. Stockton, California, is the nearest town (*is* there a Stockton, California?) and Victoria doesn't actually have much to do other than deal with the week's crisis—she simply *is,* like God Herself. Her savvy, nobody's-fool portrayal of a woman so decent she accepts her deceased husband's orphaned love child as her own is, well, rousing and believable, but more on that later. She sweeps down the Barkleys' *Beauty and the Beast* staircase in rustling, high-necked satin or rides her horse side-saddle, a little bolero hat perched sideways on her perfectly coifed white hair. She's good to everyone, particularly the downtrodden, and her children call her Mother without a trace of irony. They consult her, they sometimes listen to her, they protect her when necessary. When she rescues them, driving hijacked buckboards full of dynamite here and there to save them the trouble, they applaud her efforts with good-humored brio. They like their mother! What a concept! As the age of Aquarius dawned in the real world and all hell broke loose, the shell-shocked mothers of teenagers may well have formed a healthy, so to speak, portion of the show's fans.

But back to our story. Jarrod, the eldest son, played by Richard Long, is an urbane lawyer in his early thirties who can ride a horse when called upon but dresses in string ties and suits. Obviously the brightest male bulb in the Barkley manse, he manages the family legal affairs and has an ironic, Bond-like glint in his eye. Strangely, though, he doesn't often exercise his sexual élan on-camera and lives part-time in San Francisco. Hmm. For whatever reason, the women mostly fight over Nick and Heath. Nick Barkley, played by Peter Breck, manages the ranch itself and specializes in striding across rooms, his gun belt slung low around his hips. He's an unapologetic brunette hothead with a sense of humor who competes openly with Heath, the blond youngest brother who appears out of nowhere to elicit protective instincts in any female with a beating heart. If Nick isn't fighting *with* Heath à la *Sons and Lovers* in a boxing ring, exhibition-style, for the pleasure of the townsfolk on July 4, he's fighting to defend Heath's honor. Heath's story, after all, distinguishes *The Big Valley* from the run-of-the-mill Western and forms the vulnerable core of the Barkley myth. Picture a young Lee Majors, wounded terribly by his past and looking for punishment—I mean, a home.

In "Palms of Glory," the very first episode, Heath hires on as a ranch hand after learning that Tom Barkley, deceased—remember six years before—was his father. Now, if anyone has this episode, please send it to me. "Palms of Glory," with its passing references to both Faulkner and Brontë, was flashy prime time for 1965, when handsome love children were a bit more rare in American living rooms. Heath, as it turns out, was raised in genteel poverty by his mother in a small mining town called Strawberry. He wasn't told his father's name until after his mother's death, and now has come to find his "other" family. Heath reveals his identity after Nick confronts him in a fistfight (those boys! always fighting!). The family is shocked by this revelation concerning their nearly canonized patriarch, but they refuse to turn Heath away. He stays on at the ranch, proving himself brave and stalwart the next week. A third episode finds Victoria journeying to Strawberry to learn more. How could Tom have truly loved her if he fathered a child with another woman? Evidence comes to light: A letter written by Tom Barkley to Heath's mother reveals that she discovered him beaten almost to death in an alley and nursed him back to health. Her tender, loving care led to her pregnancy with Heath, but the letter made clear that Tom never knew of Heath's existence. Tom, his health (and perhaps his memory?) restored, returned to hearth and home. Heath's mother, in the tradition of proud, independent women, never asked for a dime or told Tom Barkley he had another good-looking heir. They exchanged letters of closure and she accepted Tom's status as a happily married patriarch, apparently swore off men forever, and raised Heath with the help of two women friends. Hmm; was she bisexual? Forget I asked. Her pride was hard on Heath, who knocked around early enough (we learn in a much later episode) that he was imprisoned at Carterson, a fictional Civil War prison camp, at the tender age of thirteen. Heath starts the series as an Angry Young Man but progresses to Strong, Silent Type as he draws closer to the family fold, while the Barkleys prove themselves the ultimate functional family. They take in and protect the outsider love child, thereby ennobling everyone involved. Heath's illegitimate status remains an issue to various small-minded antagonists, but the family deals with them together, providing emotionally satisfying, broad-minded grist for the weekly mill.

In "Winner Lose All" (Season 1, Episode 7, for those who are keeping count), Katharine Ross plays Maria Montera, beautiful only child of Don Alfredo Montera, an aristocratic Mexican rancher with whom the Barkleys are involved in a land dispute. She falls in love with Heath, who reveals his true past to her as they lie in a fully clothed embrace under a cottonwood tree: "You call it, I've been there. You name it, I've done it." A truly Whitmanesque wanderer, he catalogs a quick song of himself: digging for gold on the mother lode, fishing for salmon off the Golden

Gate, riding shotgun on a stagecoach, scouting Apaches for a wagon train. The lovely Maria wonders aloud why he had to work so hard when his father was so wealthy, and innocently observes that he looks like his mother. "You never saw my mother," Heath retorts bitterly. "Tom Barkley and my mother were never married, and you don't have to look if the light's too strong." Ross observes with sincere therapeutic candor (more recently displayed in her turn as Jake Gyllenhaal's psychiatrist in *Donnie Darko*) that the light's just right. Heath's still perfect in her eyes, if a bit short-tempered.

Her father, however, doesn't agree, providing Victoria Barkley with one of her classiest scenes. Don Alfredo comes calling and proposes they marry Maria off to Nick, legitimate Barkley heir, while Victoria sends Heath away for a year. After all, Don Alfredo insists, children "forget so quickly." Victoria doesn't dignify the suggestion with consideration. "Forgive me, Don Alfredo," she says, fixing him with her flinty, gemlike gaze, "but I always rest at this time. Silas will see you out." She turns on her heel and walks away, up that staircase, head held high while he sputters and fumes, brushing past the equally unruffled Silas. Silas, played with aplomb by Napoleon Whiting, merely raises his brows in silent comment.

In the end, Maria defies her father, who gives in at a crucial moment and admits his mistake. She follows her father's wishes and forswears Heath, but leaves both men in the final scene, riding that stagecoach back east to nurse her broken heart. Fealty to family conquers all and everyone stays single. On to the next episode!

I was nearly sixteen when *The Big Valley* ended. By 1968 the Tet Offensive was raging; I stopped watching much TV, other than graphic news footage in which a confused America confronted the realities of the dream. If my friends and I paid any attention to *The Big Valley*, we might have joked that Heath and Victoria, as the only family on the show not actually blood-related, should really get together. Or noted that Silas, the dignified, finely made black butler, was approximately Victoria's age and height, and appeared to be the only one in the house (remember, Jarrod was usually in San Francisco) intelligent enough to carry on a conversation with her. We might have wondered why Silas, who appeared to have a room upstairs like the rest of the family, seemingly comprised the entire domestic staff of a ranch the size of Rhode Island. Now, there was a man with boundless energy! We might have mused about the connection between *The Big Valley* and matriarchy, and attached a certain anatomical relevance to the name of the show. We'd heard about free love and earth mothers and Woodstock. Wealthy widowhood and strait-laced manners to burn no longer seemed attractive. Class, as in a mode of behavior, was elitist, wasn't it? Class wasn't enough in Selma, or in Haiphong Harbor. Class didn't win *Roe vs. Wade,* but class did allow women to preserve their dignity and espouse their own ideals despite crisis and the daily grind. *The Big Valley* spoke volumes to girls growing up, girls who watched their mothers manage much smaller domains with little help and less thanks. The actual Big Valley, it seemed, was the one women walked through. Victoria Barkley raised faithful sons and an apple-cheeked girl to walk with her, but she was the one who kept it all going, standing there under a sky as big and smooth as a glossy, miles-wide dinner plate.

Where I came from, the skies were not that big. Valleys we understood, and forks and runs, as in dirt roads that meander along the course of streams and creeks. In 1965, my mother taught first grade at the same elementary school her three children attended. Once a week we picked up the ironing from Peg Hogan, a tall, rangy woman of indeterminate age who wore glasses and smoked cigarettes with calm nonchalance. Peg set the world straight with salty, dismissive comments while my mother hung my father's shirts and her own Peter Pan–collared blouses on a hook in our turquoise Mercury. The easy camaraderie between the two women belied the fact that my mother, one of the few in her circle who needed to work and did, paid a woman who earned even less than she to do her ironing. My mother was nearly forty. Peg may have been fifty or sixty. At twelve I didn't think much about how old they were, but I already recognized in both women the level gaze, the wry set of the mouth, the "Pour it on, I can take it" attitude of women who ran their own shows and paid their own bills. I don't know if Peg was a *Big Valley* fan, and I don't recall that my mother took much time to watch TV, but their Monday-afternoon encounters seemed an expression of the same decency Victoria Barkley embodied as she directed events and kept the ranch afloat against all odds. Class as character had nothing to do with money, lineage, or historical era, and it often comprised the only weapon available to women. There they stood, Peg with her laundry baskets and sacks of hangers, my mother with her chunky pencils, phonics texts, and reams of wide-lined vanilla paper, in direct contrast to the fairy tales popular culture represented as women's lives.

The Big Valley has vanished into the mists of eBay, and none of us is twelve anymore. If the show encouraged its own fairy tale, a world in which loyalty to wise parental authority was always rewarded, *The Big Valley* seems memorable now for Stanwyck's classy response to a real-life dilemma. A fine actress, midlife in an era of limitations, she made the most of the opportunity allowed her and infused four seasons of fantasy with her hands tied behind her back.

THE WOUND and the BOW

David Shields

I know that Howard Cosell was childishly self-absorbed and petulant ("It's hard to describe the rage and frustration you feel, both personally and professionally, when you are vilified in a manner that would make Richard Nixon look like a beloved humanitarian. You can't imagine what it does to a person until you've experienced it yourself, especially when you know that the criticism is essentially unfair"); that he would obsess upon, say, the *Dubuque Courier*'s critique of his performance ("What's a Dubuque courier?" his colleague once replied); that too soon after he achieved prominence, the beautiful balance between righteous anger and comic self-importance got lost and he was left only with anger and self-importance; that he once said that he, along with Walter Cronkite and Johnny Carson, was one of the three great men in the history of American television; that he mercilessly teased his fellow *Monday Night Football* announcers, Frank Gifford and Don Meredith, but pouted whenever they teased him; that he was certain he should have been a network anchor and/or a U.S. Senator; that the very thing he thought needed deflating—the "importance of sports"—he was crucially responsible for inflating; that after hitching a ride on boxing and football for decades, he then turned around and dismissed them when he no longer needed them ("The NFL has become a stagnant bore"; "I'm disgusted with the brutality of boxing"); that, in an attempt to assert his (nonexistent) expertise, he would frequently excoriate any rookie who had the temerity to commit an egregious error on *Monday Night Football* (dig the Cosellian diction); that he was a shameless name-dropper of people he barely knew; that he said about a black football player, "That little monkey gets loose," then, regarding the brouhaha that ensued, said, "They're conducting a literary pogrom against me"; that *New York Times* sports columnist Red Smith once said, "I have tried hard to like Howard Cosell, and I have failed"; that legendary sportswriter Jimmy Cannon said about him, "This is a guy who changed his name [from Cohane to Cosell], put on a toupee, and tried to convince the world he tells it like it is"; that David Halberstam said he bullied anyone who disagreed with him; that he frequently boasted about *Monday Night Football*, "We're bigger than the game"; that he once told a Senate subcommittee, "I'm a unique personality who has had more impact upon sports broadcasting in America than any person who has yet lived"; that he once wrote, "Who the hell made *Monday Night Football* unlike any other sports program on the air? If you want the plain truth, I did"; that at the height of his fame when fans would come up to him on the street to kibitz or get an autograph, he liked to turn to whomever he was with and say (seriously? semi-seriously?), "Witness the adulation"; that when Gene Upshaw, head of the NFL Players Association, said about Cosell, "His footprints are in the sand," he corrected the compliment: "My footprints are cast in stone."

I know all of that and don't really care, because for a few years—1970 to 1974, the first four years it was on the air, when I was in high school—*Monday Night Football* mattered deeply to me, and it mattered because of Cosell. I haven't watched more than a few minutes of any *MNF* game since then, and at the time I had no real coherent sense of its significance, but looking back, I would say it's not an exaggeration to claim that Howard Cosell changed my life, maybe even—in at least one sense—saved it. *MNF* was "Mother Love's traveling freak show" (Meredith's weirdly perfect description), a "happening" (Cosell's revealingly unhip attempt to be hip); it was the first sports broadcast to feature three sportscasters, nine cameras, shotgun mikes in the stands and up and down and around the field. Celebrities showed up in the booth: Nixon told Gifford he wished he had become a sportscaster instead of a politician; John Lennon told Cosell that he became a troublemaker because people didn't like his face (Cosell's comment afterward: "I know the feeling"); Cosell stood next to Bo Derek and said with pitch-perfect, mock self-pity that here was a classic case of Beauty and the Beast; Cosell told John Wayne that he was a terrible singer and the Duke agreed; after Cosell interviewed Spiro Agnew, Meredith said that what no one knew was that Agnew was wearing a Howard Cosell wristwatch. This was all cool and droll. It was all finally just show biz, though. What wasn't was Cosell's relation, as an artist, to his material (I use the terms advisedly): "By standing parallel to the game and owing nothing to it, by demystifying it, by bullying it and not being bullied by it—by regarding the game as primarily an entertainment, though realizing also the social forces that impact on it—I was able to turn *Monday Night Football* into an Event, and I do mean to use the capital E. Now it is part of American pop culture, and if it sounds like my ego is churning on overdrive for taking the lion's share of credit for it, then I'll take the mane."

I grew up in the sixties and seventies in suburban San Francisco, the son of left-wing Jewish journalist-activists. My mother was the public information officer for one of the first desegregated school districts in California. One day the human-relations consultant informed her that the revolution wouldn't occur until white families gave up their houses in the suburbs and moved into the ghetto. My mother tried for the better part of the evening to convince us to put our house up for sale. One Easter weekend at Watts Towers, my mother looked smogward through some latticed wine bottles with a positively religious sparkle in her dark eyes. When my cousin Sarah married a black man from Philadelphia, Sarah's mother wasn't able to attend, so my mother substituted and brought the temple down with an a cappella finale of "Bridge Over Troubled Water." My father held dozens of jobs, but perhaps the one he loved the most was director of the San Mateo poverty program during the late sixties. He sat in a one-room office without central heating and called grocery stores, wanting to know why they didn't honor food stamps; called restaurants, asking if, as the sign in the windows proclaimed, they were indeed equal-opportunity employers. Sometimes, on weekends, he flew to Sacramento or Washington to request more money for his program. Watts rioted, Detroit burned. My father said, "Please, I'm just doing my job." He got invited to barbecues, weddings, softball games. The salary was $7,500 a year, but I never saw him happier.

No one ever had his or her heart more firmly fixed in the right place than my father and mother, with the possible exception of Howard Cosell. Traveling in a limo through a tough part of Kansas City on the way to the airport after a game, he told the driver, Peggy, to stop the car when he saw two young black men fighting each other, surrounded by a group of guys cheering for blood. Cosell got out and instantaneously was the ringside announcer: "Now, I want you to listen here. It's quite apparent to this observer that the young southpaw doesn't have a jab. And you, my friend, over here, you obviously do not have the stamina to continue. This conflict is halted posthaste." Handshakes, autographs. When Cosell got back in the limo and Peggy expressed her astonishment at what she'd just seen, Cosell leaned back, took a long drag on his cigar, and said, "Pegeroo, just remember one thing: I know who I am." Which, according to him, was "a man of causes. My entire professional life has been predicated upon making the good fights, the fights that I believe in. And much of the time it was centered around the black athlete. My real fulfillment in broadcasting has always come from crusading journalism, fighting for the rights of people such as Jackie Robinson, Muhammad Ali, and Curt Flood. The greatest influence of my life was Jackie Roosevelt Robinson [the inevitable name-drop], certainly one of my closest friends." My father rooted for the Dodgers because they were originally from Brooklyn and then moved to Los Angeles, just as he was and had, but we as a clan stayed loyal to them because they hired the first black baseball player (Jackie Robinson), retained the first crippled black baseball player (Roy Campanella), and started the highest number of nice-seeming black players (Johnny Roseboro, Jim Gilliam, Tommy Davis, et al.). *New York Post* sportswriter Maury Allen said, "The single most significant issue in the twentieth century was race, and Howard Cosell was unafraid about race."

Cosell defended Ali when he refused to serve in Vietnam following his conversion to Islam. When Cosell died, Ali said, "Howard Cosell was a good man and he lived a good life. I can hear Howard now saying, 'Muhammad, you're not the man you used to be ten years ago.'" Ali was referring to Cosell standing up at a pre-fight conference and saying to him, "Many people believe you're not the man you used to be ten years ago." Ali replied, "I spoke to your wife, and she said you're not the man you were *two* years ago." Cosell giggled like a schoolboy. Asked once what he stood for, Cosell replied, "I stood for the Constitution, in the case of *The U.S. versus Muhammad Ali*. What the government did to this man was inhuman and illegal under the Fifth and Fourteenth Amendments. Nobody says a damned word about the professional football players who dodged the draft. But Muhammad was different. He was black and he was boastful. Sportscasters today aren't concerned with causes and issues. Can you see any of those other guys putting their careers on the line for an Ali?" According to Cosell's daughter Jill, he frequently said that if people didn't stand up for things, they weren't good for much else.

Music to my parents' Marxist ears. As was this: "The importance that our society attaches to sports is incredible. After all, is football a game or a religion? The people of this country have allowed sports to get completely out of hand." And this: "The sports world is an ever-spinning spiral of deceit, immorality, absence of ethics, and defiance of the public interest." And this: "There's got to be a voice such as mine somewhere, and I enjoy poking my stick at various issues and passersby." And this: "For myself, I wondered when someone other than me would tell the truth." And this: "What was it all about, Alfie? Was football that important in this country? Was it a moral crime to introduce objective commentary to the transmission of a sports event?"—after he'd been pilloried in Cleveland for saying that Browns running back Leroy Kelly hadn't been a "compelling factor" in the first half of the first *MNF* game (he hadn't). "If so, how did we as a people get this way? In the spoon-fed, Alice in Wonderland world of sports broadcasting, the public was not accustomed to hearing its heroes questioned." When, following his eulogy of Bobby Kennedy on his *Speaking of Sports* show and fan after fan called in to complain—"Don't tell me how to live—just give us the scores. That's what you're paid for"—Cosell said, "I began to wonder if that kind of thinking is one of the things that makes us so prone to assassination in this country. Maybe there is such an absence of intellect and sensitivity that only violence is understandable and acceptable." "The 'fan,'" Cosell pointed out, "is a telephone worker, a transit worker, a power-company worker, a steelworker, a teacher, whatever. He has never given up the right to strike and often does. When he does the public is inconvenienced and sometimes the public health and safety are threatened. When a ballplayer strikes, the effect upon public health and safety is nil. Nor is public convenience disturbed, for that matter. Yet the ballplayer and the owner are called upon to each give up their individual bargaining rights because the 'fan' wants baseball and 'is entitled to get it.'" "I never played the game with advertisers, with my own company, or with the sports operators," Cosell said. "And, of course, I never played the game as a professional athlete."

This is where it gets complicated, because I was a monomaniacal, five-foot-four, 120-pound freshman basketball player at Aragon High School in San Mateo who, somehow, was supremely confident that he was destined to become a professional athlete.

From kindergarten to tenth grade all I really did was play sports, think about sports, dream about sports. I learned how to read by devouring mini-bios of jock stars. I learned math by computing players' (and my own) averages. When I was twelve I ran the fifty-yard dash in six seconds, which caused kids from all over the city to come to my school and race me. During a five-on-five weave drill at a summer basketball camp, the director of the camp, a recently retired basketball player, got called over to watch how accurately I could throw passes behind my back; he said he could have used a point guard like me when he was playing, and he bumped me up out of my grade level. I remember once hitting a home run in the bottom of the twelfth inning to win a Little League All-Star game and then coming home to lie down in my uniform in the hammock in our backyard, drink lemonade, eat sugar cookies, and measure my accomplishments against the fellows featured in the just-arrived issue of *Sports Illustrated*. Christ, I remember thinking, how could life possibly get any better than this?

In junior high I would frequently take the bus crosstown, toss my backpack under my father's desk, and spend the rest of the afternoon playing basketball with black kids. I played in all seasons and instead of other sports. In seventh grade I developed a double-pump jump shot, which in seventh grade was almost unheard of. Rather than shooting on the way up, I tucked my knees, hung in the air a second, pinwheeled the ball, then shot on the way down. My white friends hated my new move. It seemed tough, mannered, teenage, vaguely Negro. The more I shot like this, the more my white friends disliked me, and the more they disliked me, the more I shot like this. At the year-end assembly, I was named Best Athlete, and my mother said that when I got up to accept the trophy, I even walked like a jock. At the time I took this as the ultimate accolade, though I realize now she meant it as a gentle mockery.

My father didn't particularly mind my mindlessness, since, in addition to being director of the poverty program, he was also a lifelong athlete (runner, swimmer, trophy-winning tennis player) and sporadic sportswriter who, even now, at ninety-two, still writes an occasional sports column for the local suburban California weekly. My mother, on the other hand, disapproved. Once, she said to me, "Sometimes when people ask me if all you ever do is play sports, I want to tell them, 'At least he's devoted to something. At least he has an activity at which he excels,' but other times I wish you were obsessed with something a little more permanent."

"Yes, I know," I whispered; it was very late on some Sunday night.

"Sometimes I just want to tell those people, 'Leave me alone. Leave him alone. He's like a dancer on that damn playfield or ball yard or what have you.' But what I usually tell them, what I really feel, and what I guess I'm trying to tell you now is that I wish you'd dedicate yourself with the same passion to a somewhat more elevated calling."

"Yes, I know," I whispered again, turning and trotting off to sleep.

Sports and politics have always been, for me, in curiously close conversation, alliance, overlap, competition. None of the kids I played sports with were Jewish. They called me Buddha Boy (I never quite understood this moniker—Judaism was as unfathomable to them as Buddhism?) and Ignatz (my body was small and my ears were large), and asked me why anyone would want to be Jewish. When Sandy Koufax refused to pitch during the World Series, I suddenly felt proud to stay home on Yom Kippur. My father derives his identity at least as much from Jewish boxers and basketball players from the 1930s and Hank Greenberg as he does from his P.S. 149 schoolmates Danny Kaye and Phil Silvers.

In high school I was athletic and thus, to a certain extent, popular. However, I worked unduly hard at sports, with very little *sprezzatura*, which made me extremely unpopular among the really popular, really athletic people. Why? Because I made popularity or grace look like something less than a pure gift. Only the really popular, really athletic people knew I was unpopular, so I could, for instance, be elected, if I remember correctly, vice president of the sophomore class and yet be, in a sense, underappreciated.

Cosell, who knew the feeling, amplified. "I remember going to school in the morning," he said in his *Playboy* interview. "A Jewish boy. I remember having to climb a back fence and run because the kids from St. Theresa's parish were after me. My drive, in a sense, relates to being Jewish and living in an age of Hitler. I think these things create insecurities in you that live forever." As if in proof of these insecurities, he said, "I am the most hated man on the face of the earth."

Still, he did have a point. He was voted most disliked sportscaster of the 1970s. One sign at a stadium said WILL ROGERS NEVER MET HOWARD COSELL. Another sign said HOWARD IS A HEMORRHOID. A contest was held: The winner got to throw a brick through a TV set when Cosell was talking. Buddy Hackett told Johnny Carson, "There are two schools of thought about Howard Cosell. Some people hate him like poison, and some people just hate him regular."

One Saturday night, two medics carrying a stretcher stormed my family's front door, looking for someone who had supposedly fallen on the front steps. Later the next afternoon, a middle-aged man, slightly retarded, tried to deliver a pepperoni pizza. A cop came to investigate a purported robbery. Another ambulance. A florist. An undertaker from central casting. Vehicles from most areas of the service sector were, at one point, parked virtually around the block. I was certain, though I could never prove it, that my popular, athletic friends, who always gathered together to watch the proceedings with binoculars in one of their houses at the top of the hill, had orchestrated all this traffic. Every Halloween I cowered in my basement bedroom with the doors locked, lights out, shades down, and listened to the sound of lobbed eggs.

I had company. "Cosell, the Mouth, why don't you drop dead? There's a bomb in Rich Stadium. It will blow you up at ten P.M., Monday." "If he comes to Green Bay on October 1, I'm going to kill him, and your sheriff's department can't stop me." "You will die now, because your government lies. I will be out in October and will be there to get you and all ABC government cheaters."

The death threats always came from smaller, less cosmopolitan towns or cities—Buffalo; Green Bay; Milwaukee; Denver: Deer Lodge, Montana—whose residents must have thought Cosell seemed like Sissified Civilization itself.

Every plot needs a villain, as Bill Cosby told Cosell. Cosell says that when they were struggling through the first rehearsal of *MNF*, he reassured Meredith: "The Yankee lawyer and the Texas cornpone, putting each other on. You'll wear the white hat, I'll wear the black hat, and you'll have no problems from the beginning. You're going to come out of this a hero. I know this country. There's nothing this country loves more than a cowboy, especially when he's standing next to a Jew. Middle America will love you. Southern America will love you. And there are at least forty sportswriters in the country who can't wait to get at me. You'll benefit thereby. Don't worry about me, though. Because in the long run it will work out for the old coach, too." Which it did, at least for a while, for longer than anyone thought possible.

Gifford was the fair-haired Hall-of-Famer. "People always looked for things in me they'd like to see in themselves," Gifford claimed. "I've never known what to think of it." Ah, but he did. "Look at him standing there, girls," Cosell liked to say within earshot of Gifford at meet-and-greets before *MNF* games. "A veritable Greek god. America's most famous football hero. The dream of the American working girl. The single most sexually dynamic man in the chronicle of the male sex." Cosell was up for this jocularity; so, in a way, was Gifford (in his memoir *The Whole Ten Yards*, he gleefully quotes his wife, Kathie Lee, calling him a "love machine").

"Anyone who looked like Ichabod Crane and spoke with a nasal Brooklyn accent didn't exactly fit the sportscaster mold," Gifford said later about Cosell, in retaliation. "On top of that, Howard was Jewish."

"Of course there are critics," Cosell sighed one night on *MNF*. "There will always be critics. 'The dogs bark, but the caravan rolls on.'" Meredith—good ole boy with a slight sideways wit—said, "Woof."

A receiver muffed an easy catch, and Meredith said, "Hey, he should be on *Saturday Night Live with Howard Cosell*," which tanked after twelve shows. Cosell glowered.

Gifford, Meredith, and Cosell couldn't find anywhere to eat late one night, so the limo pulled into a McDonald's in a slum. Meredith urged Cosell to exit: "Ha'hrd, they want you. It's your constituency. You know, the poor, the downtrodden. You're always taking about them. Shit, Ha'hrd, here they are!"

Once, when the Giants were playing the Cowboys on *MNF*, Cosell said, teasingly, that he wasn't impressed by the play of Meredith's and Gifford's (former) respective teams, and Meredith replied, "At least we have respective teams."

Cosell should have laughed, but he didn't. I should have laughed when my faux-friends made fun of me, but I didn't, I couldn't (and so they made more fun of me). Cosell was/I was . . . everything they weren't: Jewish, verbal, performative, engagé, contrarian, pretentious but insecure, despising (adoring) athletics and athletes.

Instead, Cosell would tattle to *MNF* executive producer Roone Arledge: "They're doing it again. The two jocks are out to get me. They're after me again."

Instead, Cosell said to Meredith, "Don't start it because you don't stand a chance. Get into a duel of words with me, and I'll put you away."

Instead, he said about Gifford, "He admired my command of the language, my ability to communicate, and he was shrewd enough not to engage me in a debate. He had to know he couldn't win."

Witness the adulation of words. For Cosell, language was everything, as All-American Heroism was/is for Gifford (this all blew away in a storm when scandal hit Gifford's marriage and his career came undone; we're in Cheever country—the perfect Connecticut house is no bulwark against the crooked timber of humanity) and Texan joie de vivre was/is for Meredith (this, too, was a crock; Meredith came to despise the "Dandy Don" mask that was his meal ticket). Once, on air, Meredith kissed Cosell on the cheek, pretending to gag on Cosell's toupee. Cosell immediately responded by saying, "I didn't know you . . . cared." The way he paused before saying the word "cared," and the pressure that he put on the word, thrilled me to the bottom of my fifteen-year-old toes. "You're being extremely . . . truculent," he admonished Muhammad Ali once, and again, it was the way he paused before "truculent" and the extraordinary torque he put on the word so that he seemed to be simultaneously brandishing it as a weapon and mocking his own sesquipedalianism. In *The Whole Ten Yards,* Gifford, surely leaning more than a little on his cowriter, *Newsweek* television writer Harry Waters, says about Cosell: "His genius lay in turning his liabilities into assets. He gave his voice"—thick New Yawk honk, full of Brooklyn bile—"a dramatic, staccato delivery that grabbed you by the ears." I, too, wanted to turn my liabilities into strengths. I knew what my liabilities were; only what were my strengths?

I had been aware since I was six or seven that I stuttered, but the problem would come and go; it never seemed that serious or significant. I had successfully hid out from it, or it from me. Now, as a sophomore in high school, with my hormones trembling, my lips were, too. In class, I'd sit in back, pretending not to hear when called upon, and, when pressed to respond, would produce an answer I knew was incorrect but was the only word I could say. I devotedly studied the dictionary and thesaurus in the hope I could possess a vocabulary of such immense range that for every word, I'd know half a dozen synonyms and thus always be able to substitute an easy word for an unspeakable one. My sentences became so saturated with approximate verbal equivalents that what I thought often bore no relation to what I actually said.

One day I was asked whether the origin of the American Revolution was essentially economic or philosophical. I wanted to say, as my mother and father had taught me, that revolution arises from an unfair distribution of wealth, but instead I replied, "The Whigs had a multiplicity of fomentations, ultimate or at least penultimate of which would have to be their predilection to be utterly discrete from colonial intervention, especially on numismatical pabulae." The teacher looked down at his desk. The class roared. By the end of the week I'd been scheduled to meet with the school's speech therapist.

She was very pretty but not especially my type: a little too cherubic to be truly inspiring. Miss Acker knew I was a basketball player and proved to be surprisingly knowledgeable about the game, so for the first half hour we talked about how it doesn't matter if a guard is short if he knows how to protect the ball; what a shame it was the high school had no girls' basketball team; how *A Sense of Where You Are* was good but *The Last Loud Roar* was probably even better.

Then she had to turn on the tape recorder, hand me a mimeographed memorandum, and say, "You've been speaking really well, Dave—only a few minor disfluencies here and there. Let me hear you read for a while."

"Oh, I read fine," I said, and wasn't being intentionally insincere. I saw myself as a relatively articulate reader.

"That's funny," she said, and started rummaging around in her drawer for something or other. "Almost all stutterers have at least a little trouble when it comes to reading out loud."

I, on the other hand, disliked the label. It sounded like *atheist* or *heretic* or *cat burglar*.

"I don't see myself exactly as a stutterer," I said. "It's more just a case of getting nervous in certain situations. When I feel comfortable, I never have any trouble talking."

This wasn't true, but I felt pressed.

"Well, you feel comfortable with me, I hope. Why don't you read aloud that memo? We'll record it, play it back, and you can tell me what you think."

At the time, my particular plague happened to be words beginning with vowels. This text, for one reason or another, was riddled with them. I kept opening my mouth and uttering air bubbles, half-human pops of empty repetition. Miss Acker didn't have to play the tape back for me to know it had been the very embodiment of babble, but she did, and then, raising her right eyebrow, asked, "Well?"

I explained that the whirring of the tape recorder and her ostentatious tallying of my errata had made me nervous. The proof I wasn't just one more stutterer was that I could whisper.

"But, Dave," she said, "that's characteristic of stutterers."

"That's not true," I said. "You're lying. I know you are. You're just saying that. Stutterers cannot whisper. I know they can't."

"Yes they can," she said. "Virtually all stutterers can whisper. You're a stutterer. I want you to admit that fact. It's an important step. Once you acknowledge it, we can get to work on correcting it. When you're a professional basketball player, I don't want to see you giving hesitant interviews at halftime."

The flattery tactic didn't work the second time, not least because she was wrong: As Howard Cosell well knew, the athletic aesthetic is always to assert that the ecstasies experienced by the body are beyond the reach of words, whereas to some cerebral people, unfortunately, the primal appeal of a warrior-athlete is incalculable. I'd regularly distinguished myself from the common run of repeaters by the fact that I could whisper; now, informed I was one among millions, I was enraged—at what or whom I didn't quite know, but enraged.

I stood and said, "I don't want your happy posters or your happy smiles or your happy basketball chitchat. I don't want to be happy. I want to be u-u-unusual." Then I did something I thought was very unusual: I tore down a poster of a seagull and ran out of the room. Having never before confronted myself and found myself in any real way wanting, I returned to her office the next day and began what—thirty years later—still feels like my life: a life limited but also defined by language.

Within a week, Miss Acker got me switched out of Typing and into Public Speaking. The Speech teacher, Mr. Roshoff, by far the most charismatic teacher in the school, had been the object of my older sister's (and many other girls') crush for years. He was tall and lean and witty and bottomlessly, brutally ironic in a way that seemed not entirely dissimilar to Cosell's manner. Every week or so, we had to present a new speech, and with these I suffered predictably, but then I hit on the idea of doing a speech imitating Cosell. This was 1972—fall, the first month of my sophomore year, the second year of *MNF*—and so I went to school the only way I could on "The Mouth," without the aid of a VCR, which was more than a decade away: I simply watched him and thought about him as much as I could, even more than I had before.

"The Mouth" was a good nickname for him. He was such an insatiably oral guy, talking nonstop—the way my mother and sister and Mr. Roshoff did—and always pouring liquor down his throat and jamming a huge stogie in his mouth. Dick Ebersol, now president of NBC Sports, said about Cosell, "He was defined by what he said, not how he looked or spoke." As with virtually everything Dick Ebersol has ever said, this is exactly wrong. How he looked and how he spoke were everything. With his pasty skin, his stoop-shoulder walk, his ridiculous toupee, his enormous ears and schnoz, he always reminded me of nothing so much as a very verbose and Jewish elephant. The sportswriter Frank Deford's paean to him nicely conveys this quality: "He is not the one with the golden locks [Gifford] or the golden tan [Meredith], but the old one, shaking, sallow, and hunched, with a chin whose purpose is not to exist as a chin but only to fade so that his face may, as the bow of a ship, break the waves and not get in the way of that voice." The things he could do with that voice: the way, every week at halftime on *MNF,* he would extemporize the NFL high-lights in that roller-coaster rhetoric of his and, in so doing, "add guts and life to a damned football game," as he said, or as Chet Forte, executive director of *MNF* for years and years, said later, "It's not a damn football game. It's a show. That's what those guys [Gifford and Meredith] never understood. They never appreci-ated what Howard did. He could make two eighty-five-year-olds playing a game of marbles sound like the most exciting event in the history of sports." He had found a way to be better than what he was reporting on, to bully reality, to make life into language.

After a week of practice, I had my Cosell imitation down. Stutterers typically don't stutter when singing, whispering, acting, or imitating someone else, and when I did my Cosell imitation, I didn't stutter. I was melodramatically grandiloquent and enter-taining in the Cosellian vein. Everyone in the class loved my per-formance—it ended with the football purportedly landing in and thereby shutting my/Cosell's mouth—and Mr. Roshoff loved it, too. For the next three years, he rarely passed me without saying softly, out of the side of his mouth, "HEL-lo, every-BODY, this is HOW-wud Co-SELL." It was easy to see why my sister and several of her friends had crushes on him. Still, I could imitate

Howard Cosell; so what? So could and did a lot of other people. Where did that get me, exactly?

Toward the end of my sophomore year—Mother's Day, actually—I went to the beach with my mother. After a while she dozed off, so I walked along the shore until I was invited to join a game of Tackle the Guy with the Ball. After I scored several times in a row, several players ganged up to tackle the guy with the ball (me) and down I went. Suddenly my left leg was tickling my right ear, the water was lapping at my legs, and a crowd of about a hundred people gathered around me to speculate as to whether I was permanently paralyzed. Bursting through the throng, my mother threw up her hands and wailed at me, "See? See what sports will do to you?" She was very sympathetic later on, but her first reaction was, approximately, "I told you so."

I had a badly broken leg—my left femur—and was in traction the entire summer, but when the doctors misread the X ray and removed the body cast too early, I had to have a pin inserted in my leg and had to use a leg brace and crutches my entire junior year. I still stutter slightly, but in high school my stutter was so severe that it effectively defined who I was. My whole life was structured around the idea of doing one thing so well that people forgave me for, and I forgave myself for, my "disfluency" (Miss Acker's term). With the jockocracy newly closed to me, I became, nearly overnight, an insanely overzealous chess player, carried along by the aftermath of the Fischer-Spassky World Championship. I got to the point that I dreamt in chess notation, but I was certainly never going to become a chess whiz, and I rationalized to myself that if one could be, as Bobby Fischer was, the best chess player in the world but still a monster and a moron, the game wasn't interesting and so I abandoned it after several months, joining the school paper.

By my senior year I had recovered well enough from my broken leg that I was twelfth man on the varsity basketball team and second doubles in tennis, but sports no longer meant much to me. All that physical expression had gone inside; language was my new channel. I suddenly loved reading; I became the editor of the paper; my parents (especially my mother) were thrilled; it was sickening. I spent no more time on my studies than I had before, but now instead of six hours a day playing sports, it was six hours a day working on the paper, writing nearly every article, taking every photograph, attending journalism conferences around the Bay Area, submitting my work to every possible high-school journalism competition, submitting the paper and my work (virtually synonymous) for competitions. My Bible was *The New Journalism,* an anthology of pieces edited by Tom Wolfe, which I read over and over again. I thought I would become a New Journalist, à la Hunter Thompson or Joan Didion.

In college, though, writing for the weekly, weakly student magazine, I got in trouble for making stuff up. Also, I was trepidatious—still—about calling people on the phone (I couldn't imitate Cosell) and so I crabwalked into creative-writing courses. I'd become a fiction writer. I'd make stuff up, and that would be okay. The only problem, as I discovered in graduate school, was that compared to other fiction writers, I'm not very interested in making stuff up. I'm much more interested in contemplating the so-called real world, including, alas, the world of sports.

I've now written several books of fiction and nonfiction, and to my astonishment and horror, half of them deal more or less explicitly with sports. My first novel concerns a sportswriter's vicarious relationship with a college basketball player. My recent book *Black Planet* is a fan's diary of an NBA season, with particular focus on how race is the true and taboo topic of the sport (hi, Mom and Dad!). Last year I compiled a book of koanlike quotations uttered by the Japanese baseball player Ichiro Suzuki. The book I'm working on now is called *Body Politic: Sport and Culture.* As my daughter says, "Daddy writes about exercise."

In *The Wound and the Bow,* Edmund Wilson analyzes how various writers, such as Dickens, Wharton, and Hemingway, used the central wound of their life as the major material of their art. Throughout her entire childhood, a writer I know worked fiendishly hard in the hope of becoming a professional ballet dancer, entering the Harkness Ballet trainee program at eighteen, but she left after less than a year. It's only right that her first book, published a couple of years ago when she was in her mid-forties, is a collection of stories set in the world of ballet, and her novel-in-progress is told from the point of view of George Balanchine. In *Rocky,* asked what he sees in dowdy Adrian, Rocky says, "She fills my gaps." I was a great child-athlete and I just assumed this play-paradise would last forever. It didn't. Writing about it fills gaps.

I wish I could say instead that the material I keep returning to is seventeenth-century Flemish painting or the Cold War or the unified field theory, but it's not. Much of what I write seems to feature an exceedingly verbal person contemplating an exceedingly physical person. I return over and over to the endlessly complex dialectic between body and mind. Whenever we talk about the body, we inevitably lie, but the body itself never lies. Our bodies always betray us—always tell us what we're really feeling (desire, fear, hatred, rapture). The body-in-motion is, for me, the site of the most meaning. At a deep spot in the river, Howard Cosell showed me the way across; he showed me where to look and, looking, how to stand.

PART THREE

THANKS FOR
BEING THERE

ROB and LAURA and the LITTLE GARAGE

Richard Bausch

We lived that first year in a little garage that had been converted into a one-bedroom furnished apartment. The narrow horizontal windows of the sealed wide door were our windows, and they ran across both the living room and the little bedroom. From the outside, it looked exactly like what it was: a garage, with a side door cut into it, at the end of a driveway next to a large white house surrounded by tall trees, oaks and sycamores and blue spruces. But inside, we had a cozy apartment with paneling and built-in bookshelves, a bright little kitchen. You came into the kitchen as you entered, and there was a small table and a refrigerator to the left, next to an opening that looked into the living room and the dining area. Past this, there was another entrance, with the bathroom to the right and the bedroom to the left. We had books everywhere, and a record player that stood on the table in the eating area because there was nowhere else to put it. There was a street lamp outside, across the driveway, and its light shone in on us like moonlight. It cast such a warm light on the first snow of that winter, and Karen woke me to see it cascading down out of the dark, building up on those narrow windows, covering us. The wind blew and made a sound that is only good if you aren't out in it—that howl of a storm on the plains. Nothing makes you feel warmer than that sound at the windows, if you *are* warm. If you have time to crawl back into bed and stay there. And when you do have time, or you make the time, it feels so good, so sweet, like all the world's best luxury, even if you have no money to speak of, and no real prospects for making any, either. Which is just how it was for us that morning. And we climbed back into bed, and called in sick, and watched *Dick Van Dyke*.

But let me go back a little.

We had a small Motorola portable television that we had bought on an impulse, coming home from our short honeymoon in May—the honeymoon had been a weekend drive down to St. Louis. We didn't especially want a TV, but all the married couples we knew owned TVs, and we supposed we ought to have one, too. The Motorola was perched on the dresser at the foot of our bed, and we'd lie there in the evenings and read and watch movies if movies were on. Some nights we sat on the sofa in the living room with a cutting board on our laps and played cards, drinking cheap wine and waiting for a pizza we'd ordered from Mr. G's, whose pizza was cheap and hot, spicy hot, and with a thin crust that was really like the crust of a pie instead of that thick bread people eat these days. TV was for those late nights when we couldn't sleep, and even then it was only if we could find a movie to watch.

This was 1969–70. I was trying to write stories, and still thinking of myself as primarily a songwriter and poet, and in fact I continued to spend long hours lying on my stomach in bed, working on what I thought were poems—mostly love poems, because of course I was in love with a very beautiful young woman and she was there with me, trying to sleep. Now and then she would stir, and say, "Honey, are you going to write all night?" And I'd kiss her and put the work down, then turn the light off and lie there, reveling in my luck, savoring it, lying with my hands clasped behind my head, looking at the moonlike light on all the surfaces in the little room and breathing in the air of happiness. That was how it felt. Sometimes it would ache, because of course I knew how quickly the world could take such happiness away. So I would revel in it, trying to be completely in the moment, and attempting to keep far from my mind the thought of ever losing it.

We were both working jobs that we treated as annoying matters to be gotten through so we could be alone together. I worked at a Walgreens, as liquor manager, which afforded me the chance to try all the various wines and whiskeys we sold. I was getting an education in the world of delightful things to imbibe other than beer, though beer was fine with me, too. She worked in the Economics Department at the University of Illinois. She worked eight to five. I worked from one in the afternoon until ten o'clock. She'd bring me dinner in the evenings, in a plastic bowl, usually with a cold beer, wrapped in a towel with ice.

In the mornings, I'd drive her to her job and then come home and try to write. I was only beginning to write stories—for a time the poems I'd written had all been narrative, though I didn't really know enough to be able to distinguish such a thing. I was very stupid about a lot of it then. So stupid that I thought it ought to be easier than it was turning out to be. I had thought that the way you did it was to write songs, like Bob Dylan, and then they would let you write novels, which is what I wanted to write, though of course I was far from being able to write anything like a novel, or near it. I was far, indeed, from being able to write a readable story, for that matter. But I was beginning, and very romantic about it, and I grew a mustache and bought a set of pencils and a stack of legal pads and spent each morning trying to work, with what little I knew, and it just got harder; and my confidence began to flag. It became more and more difficult to make myself sit down to it. I began putting it off a little, taking my time over breakfast, cleaning the apartment, getting things ready for the lunch Karen and I would have before I went on to my own job.

Worrying about the writing of fiction and wanting it to go better had begun to wear me down, to sap my energy and erode the will to wrestle with it at all. And one morning in October, I turned the television on. I'd watched plenty of it at night when I was growing up, but in the five years since I'd left home and been in, and then out of, the Air Force, I hadn't watched it at all. I hadn't even looked at the first three Super Bowls. And I had never, at any point, watched it in the daytime. But now it was noise in the morning and it diverted me, and after an hour or so of it, I would try again to write, finding out for the first time what a great motivator guilt would be in the intricacies of my habits of work. That summer, men had been to the moon, and the whole world but us, it seemed, had watched it on television. Well, now we had one, and I was using it a little like a drug.

The Dick Van Dyke Show had been off the air for three years, and I knew next to nothing about him or his show. When I had been younger I had seen him in a couple of commercials, where he had said his name in the way that I understood meant that he was among the television famous. But I had never watched the show. And except for the name of it, I hadn't ever really been aware of it *as* a show. I stumbled onto it on one of those mornings while stalling before work. The show was ending and in the credits I saw that it had been written by Carl Reiner. I knew that name quite well. As a boy, I had, along with my whole family, gotten great pleasure out of the old Sid Caesar's *Your Show of Shows*. I had a pretty thorough knowledge of the people connected with it, including Sid Caesar himself, and Carl Reiner. So, seeing the name, I marked it, and the next morning, at ten o'clock, turned the Motorola on and sat down on the foot of the bed to watch. The episode I saw was called "Coast-to-Coast Big Mouth," a late episode in the series, as it turns out. I didn't find out until many years later that Carl Reiner had appeared in several episodes as Alan Brady, without ever having his face on camera. This was one of the first ones where he actually has a visible, on-camera part. In "Coast-to-Coast Big Mouth," Rob's wife, Laura, reveals to a television quiz-show host that Alan Brady, her husband's boss, a famous television comic starring in a show much like the old Sid Caesar hour, wears a toupee. The episode ends with Reiner (Brady) sitting at his desk with a row of Styrofoam heads, each adorned with its own toupee. Laura comes into his office to apologize; he sees her, then leans into the row of heads and, looking along the line of them, addresses them: "Fellows," he says. It's one of the funniest moments I've ever seen played, anywhere. Later in that same episode, after Rob (Dick Van Dyke) comes rushing in to save his wife from the dressing-down he thinks she'll get, Brady confesses to feeling some relief that the secret is out, and Mary Tyler Moore, as Laura, says, "You mean you're happy?" Reiner (Brady) pauses, looks at her and then at Dick Van Dyke, and with a great ironical laugh says, "You see, they're perfect. Not only do we have to forgive them for their destruction, but we have to be happy about it as well." Reiner plays it so wickedly, with such relish, that it is hard to believe he isn't making it up as he goes along.

I knew, that morning, that I would watch it the following one as well. After all, this was a show about a writer. And so began a series of mornings when I would watch *Dick Van Dyke* and then set to work trying to write myself. What I was watching had no effect on what I was writing, other than to relax me, and yet don't we all, in conversation, when shows like this come up, begin to tell our favorite episodes; don't they stay with us? And the fact that Rob Petrie was a writer gave off a wonderful sense of the ordinariness of trying to make things up for a life's work. No, not the ordinariness—the honorableness. In an oddly oblique and half-conscious way, I think it helped me see that writing is not an indulgence at all; that the indulgences are what one gives up to do it in the days.

When I picked Karen up, each noon, I would tell her how the morning's work had gone, or hadn't gone, and then I would relate that morning's episode of the show. And it became a kind of talismanic thing with us, because we were like that, too—the episodes had an odd way of reminding us of each other. Well, it called up how we felt; it depicted our devotion to each other, and some of our silliness, too. For most of that winter, I watched, or we both did, but then we were moving, and we went east, to New England, and life got complicated. We were living with the family of the young friend, David Marmorstein, with whom I'd written songs through my time in the Air Force. We had traveled around the Midwest and performed, and had put together a band, and now we were trying to get something going with David's brothers and sisters. It was not going well, and Karen and I spent very little time watching any kind of TV. I wasn't writing much, either. We were in New England trying to put together this band, and I was singing and playing guitar badly and the band was coming apart, because I didn't want to do it anymore, and wasn't quite aware of it yet. I wanted to write stories, and I told Karen about it, and no one else. The band did fall apart, because David was killed in the middle of the night in an automobile accident. I started the process of applying to Boston University, and then finally, with a shock that felt like relief, understood that with David gone, nothing was holding us in New England anymore. Karen and I traveled south, where I began writing stories in earnest.

We still had very little time for much television. We watched the new *Mary Tyler Moore Show* occasionally, because we knew her from *Dick Van Dyke*. But I was in school, and we were just too busy usually to pay much attention.

It wasn't until the early nineties, when our youngest two children were just school-aged, that the cable companies began having marathons. And, of course, one of the first was of *The Dick Van Dyke Show*. We didn't have cable, but friends taped episodes for me and, since it was now playing on Nickelodeon, I had for some time been searching for it in the late nights, in hotel rooms on the road. The girls loved the show and it became a treat for us to get under the heavy blankets in the king-sized bed and watch the tapes our friends had made. We would watch three or four episodes in a row sometimes, and now and again we would fast-forward through one to get to a preferred one that we knew followed it.

It is no exaggeration to say there are parts of this old comedy—whose run was five short years, forty years ago—that my children can quote in their entirety. It has always been hard for me to realize that in fact Rob and Laura Petrie, with their house in the suburbs and their little boy, are more of my parents' generation than mine. There is something persistently contemporary-feeling about it, even with all the changes we as a country have been through. Like all great comedy, the best of the episodes stand up and are always funny, as W. C. Fields is still funny, and Laurel and Hardy, and Chaplin and Harold Lloyd and the rest.

As with those comics and comedies, we never tire of them. They keep our spirits fresh, don't they? In some strange ineffable way, they refurbish us. I don't think anything about that wonderful entertainment ever helped me write. But everything about it helped me to be less fraught, less worried about it all; it relieved stress and made me laugh. I don't believe there is any medicine for the soul more important than that. And one never writes very well when not refreshed. At least I don't.

There is also this: In some mysterious way, the whole feeling of the little family in that long-canceled television show forms some small part of our own ethos, the feeling in our house. Maybe from those early lovely days in the converted garage. Even today, when we put a tape in the machine and the theme song starts, and we settle in to watch, I get the feeling that there's snow outside, and we don't have to go anywhere, and we can put work aside for a time and relax and smile.

LIKE ROBINSON CRUSOE

Lan Samantha Chang

Desolate, my mother said. It was her first impression of the town where she would live for more than forty years. She took one step onto a pavement sheathed in ice and raised her eyes to view the narrow layer of snow-rimmed cars and houses, the edge of human evidence against the stark white sky. No people could be seen; they had stayed in against the cold. Only my father was there to welcome her. He had come weeks before, to begin his job, and now he brought my mother and sisters into the house that he had rented. It was February 1964, and my family began its life in Appleton, Wisconsin.

I have lived in seven states, on both coasts and in between, but in some vivid recess of my mind, I still believe I am a child in Appleton, sitting at the kitchen table with my mother. It is a quiet winter day. My sisters are at school and my mother is cleaning, sorting, and chopping vegetables to make the Chinese meals my father cannot do without. The outsized Midwestern green peppers are transformed to neat, bite-sized pieces in her hands. As she works, my mother describes the places she has lived. She was born in Shanghai, but her family moved two dozen times while seeking safety from the Japanese invasion and the civil war that followed. So she speaks about Chongqing, the wartime capital, sweltering in the summer heat, and she describes the constant threat of Japanese bombers. She recalls the perfect year in Hong Kong, surrounded by palm trees and the ocean's reassuring blue. Later, she lived in Shanghai on the eve of the Nationalist collapse, a time of galloping inflation, of avenues clogged with refugees on foot and bicycle and in automobiles, terrifying days light-softened in spring sun, her last glimpse of mainland China before the Communists moved into the city, driving her and my father and thousands of others to an island in the sea.

Chongqing, Shanghai. Beijing, where my father was born. These were only names to me, but they were vivid, living cities in my parents' recollections; they were the true and real world, the world left behind. My parents fled Shanghai expecting to return, but in the months after the Communist victory, the bamboo curtain tightened. Gunboats patrolled the waters. Travel ceased. Mail halted, save a trickle of letters through Hong Kong. My mother and father heard nothing from the people they had left, and the move to Appleton detached them from all family. I was born into a house of people living in exile, a tiny island of Chinese memories and customs, surrounded by vast shimmering fields of alfalfa, corn, and soybeans, by the fertile smell of dairy cows that drifted to our neighborhood on summer nights. The faraway cities, the friends my parents had known, were sealed in ice.

What does a family in exile watch on television? We had the same programs as our neighbors, but we watched them as outsiders, stealthily, seriously, spying on the culture that the TV characters revealed so easily, took for granted. We watched each joke, each gesture, and each turn of phrase. It was from television that my grandmother learned English. It was a television sitcom that

inspired my American name. My parents named me after Samantha Stephens, the domestic witch who held the power to change
her circumstances in a flash. My mother hoped that I would bring
our family such a rapid transformation.

After school, my sisters and I were permitted to watch television until dinner. Our time slot ensured us a steady diet of sitcom
reruns. I can remember a prolonged interest in *The Flintstones* and
a brief dalliance with *The Brady Bunch,* but more than anything,
we watched *Gilligan's Island.* Our repeated viewings of this show
went on for years, from grade school through junior high and into
high school. We would switch channels to catch another episode.
The show ran twice and sometimes three times daily. I must have
watched more than three thousand episodes of *Gilligan's Island*
before leaving home for college, an average of thirty viewings per
episode. For years, I found this fact embarrassing and astounding.
How was it possible that we could continue to find this old sitcom, once described by the *San Francisco Chronicle* as "a new low
in the networks' estimate of public intelligence," so endlessly ab-
sorbing? Why is *Gilligan* the one television show whose episodes
I still remember word for word?

Now, twenty years away from Appleton, our prolonged attachment to the castaways makes better sense. The brief sea trip,
the storm of change, the spinning wheel of disorientation in space
and time, were elements of our own story. The seven members of
my family—my maternal grandmother, my parents, my sisters,
and myself—lived surrounded by "native" Americans, their speech
slow, their hair blond, their customs alien. Our isolation was broken only by an occasional visit from my uncles, or a friend of the
family traveling to Chicago, guest stars stopping at our way station for a home-cooked meal and an evening of reminiscence.
When these visitors arrived, I saw my parents' past lives bloom
before them—my father's witty Mandarin puns, the unusual

snacks hand-carried from some distant Chinatown grocer—but inevitably, the visitor would leave, and we would be left alone to continue and make do.

Our cultural alienation varied according to our generation. My grandmother's homesickness was perhaps the most acute. Her age rendered her more nostalgic, less adaptive. Unlike my parents, who could look forward to a future as Americans, she had only her past in a country now closed off to her. Having reached the age when she found herself naturally turning to the past, she was obliged to reach through a geographical as well as temporal re-move. The focus of her nostalgia settled on certain missing foods. Like poor Gilligan, who squandered two of his three magic wishes on ice cream, my grandmother lay awake thinking about the dishes she had once eaten and loved: the tiny seafood dumplings in Shanghai; savory chicken wrapped in lotus leaves, a specialty of Hangzhou; the flavor of a certain pepper grown only in Sichuan. These lost dishes took on the poignancy and power of her lost youth.

My parents, plunged into a new setting in midlife, spent their time and energy adapting to the change. They settled in the new country, but knew the value of the old. Each day they ventured out to work and make our family's future; at the same time, they upheld the values of the past. They tried to make the foods my grandmother missed. They found a butcher willing to sell us the unpopular cuts she liked. They were able to re-create, with some effort, the paper-thin spring roll wrappers. Certain staples were acutely missed and difficult to make. My mother still recalls their struggles to make tofu. They drove out into the country and rang the doorbell of a soybean farmer, from whom they bought two bushels of beans (I remember the empty baskets in the garage). The traditional method required grinding, but my parents had no grinder, so they used an electric mixer to beat the soybeans into milk. They worked away at it for hours, burning up one mixer's motor in the process. My father, a chemist, devised a way to curdle soybean milk with salt. They wrapped the curds into cheesecloth and pressed it in the refrigerator. The final product was, my grandmother said, "good." Having nothing to compare it with, I was reluctant to agree.

Born in Appleton, I was doubly ignorant: I knew nothing of China, but I knew little of America outside our home. I grew up into the space between two ignorances. My confusion was profound. It never occurred to me that I found *Gilligan* soothing because its characters' lives were similar to my American life. After all, I was a native Appletonian. But I was first of all a resident of my family's island, a living museum, a repository for mixed-up cultural adaptations. I can remember watching an episode featuring the Professor's hand-cranked phonograph, then turning off the television and going outside to fly kites using a Chinese-style kite-flying reel that my father had constructed from an old telephone dial and the parts of fishing rods. I would watch the castaways serve pancake syrup made from tropical trees and then I'd sit down to a real dinner made of Southern-style "salt chicken" my parents had cured on the back porch. My grandmother, who often caught the episodes while watching over a pot of brewing ginseng roots, praised the Professor's efforts to treat Gilligan's eyes by concocting a keptibora berry extract. She said, "Sometimes homemade medicine can work better than those foreign doctors."

I was intrigued and troubled by the way that *Gilligan* preserved the shadow of my parents' war. The original series, which ran from 1964 to 1967, presented a time in which the memories of World War II's Pacific battles were not long past. In one episode, the castaways stumbled upon a hidden munitions pit. Another episode guest-starred Vito Scotti as a deranged Japanese soldier who had survived on the Pacific islands for twenty years without knowing the war had ended. This particular episode left me uneasy. I felt uncomfortable with the comical portrayal of the Asian accent, his mannerisms, and his bottle-top glasses. But I felt even more disturbed by the idea of the poor, deluded man, insisting on his own version of the war, unaware that the world had gone on without him.

Of course, time does not stand still. We were caught in its flow, through the Cold War, through feminism and Watergate. My family adapted. My mother studied American customs as carefully as she had once memorized the history of the dynasties. She kept a box of file cards listing what Americans liked to eat (large cuts of meat, sweet and sour dishes) and what they did not like (rice gruel, tofu, fish with eyes and shrimp with the shells on). She earned a second degree and became a piano teacher. My father became a Packers fan. He set up a woodworking room in the basement and made our furniture. He built standing lamps bearing the characters for longevity. He built walnut end tables with the characters for "big good luck," finished and sealed under glass.

We grew into an accomplished, noisy family with a strong sense of identity and rich blood, squeezed into a house that was too small for us. My older sisters remember us as happy, striving. But when I think of my childhood, I remember a certain sadness in the house. It stole in on the long blue shadows of our winter evenings. It was folded into the embroidered coverlets my mother kept beneath her bed. Once, while we were cleaning, my mother showed me the basement storage bin where she and my father had stacked the dusty suitcases they had brought from overseas. There, carefully wrapped in an old sheet, my father kept the long, blue silk jacket his mother had made for him when he was a young man. His mother had been left behind; he had not heard from his parents since leaving the country in 1949. This separation lay at the heart of our sadness. We were one of many families who shape this country of transplanted people, holding the long, unspoken sorrow of those cut off from what they have known.

I believe we each lived on our own island. My father enveloped himself in privacy, remembering the people he had left; my mother regretted the lost dreams of her own youth. They were not entirely unhappy; it was not so simple. They were each of them a separate being, isolated, exiled by their separate losses. I was an exile as well—not a political or geographical exile, like my parents, but a child holding on to the secret, mutinous loneliness of one who is about to leave. My island was Appleton. I did not belong in town, and there was not enough room for me to continue in our family's makeshift world. I knew that I was meant to leave our home. In a few years, I would pack my own suitcase and leave to see the world. I would come back to visit, never to stay.

But at the time, my stay in Appleton felt interminable. Each day, I would trudge home from junior high school, where I was justifiably despised for being arrogant, a "brain," awkward, and friendless. I would be in an indignant, lonely frame of mind. The drifts of snow, which seemed to fall so thickly in those days, piled high around the house, glowed violet in the deepening dusk. Inside, when I took off my coat, I could feel the cold pressing through the windows. My sisters and I would sit in the room adjacent to the kitchen and watch television with all the lights turned on. Every day, the castaways attempted a new plan to escape. They all desired to leave, the insufferable Mr. Howell and the impossible Mary Ann. I watched carefully and seldom laughed. I found the castaways' frustration unsurprising. In every episode, they tried to leave the island, and every time, their plans were foiled. No one was getting anywhere.

And then the world changed. I remember the Chinese Ping-Pong players on television. After this time of tentative outreaches, of Ping-Pong diplomacy, my oldest sister graduated and went out into the world, like a milkweed seed traveling on the wind in search of a fertile place. In September 1978, Mao died. We heard it on the evening news. My parents grew very quiet when his death was announced. I asked, "Who is Mao?" Soon afterward, my second sister left home for college. My father wrote to the mainland government for information about the whereabouts of his family. He learned their addresses and made contact with his sisters—his parents and brother had died—and in 1982 he made the long trip back through time and across the world to see them again. In 1983, I left Wisconsin to attend Thurston Howell's rival school and I stopped watching television for many years.

The world is so open now. There is an Asian grocery less than two miles from my parents' house; even the supermarkets carry tofu made with local beans. In downtown Appleton, a crowded restaurant serves authentic Chinese dishes. My parents go to Lunar New Year parties with a local Chinese club. Nor need we content ourselves with China brought to us; now we can fly there ourselves. My sister and I traveled to Beijing to meet my father's sisters. We brought back for my father his own kite-flying rod and a brightly painted silk kite shaped like a butterfly with twirling eyes. He liked the gift, although he did not use it. He has grown less sorrowful and less nostalgic, having rediscovered some old friends and reconnected with them safely, as adults. He has found a way off his island.

I have now lived away from Appleton for half my life. I moved to Connecticut, then Massachusetts, Iowa, California, New Jersey. In my travels I have not found a home. It occurs to me now, once more in Massachusetts, that I have been entirely conditioned by my childhood in the Midwest, my desires shaped to a non-specified place-longing. No sooner do I settle in one town than I begin to daydream about somewhere else. But I know there is no perfect place. It is clear that I belong not to a place but to my far-flung family, my tightly knit and fractious group of former exiles.

On a recent visit to Wisconsin, while I was sitting with my mother, an episode of *Gilligan's Island* came on. My mother and I were cutting up the vegetables for dinner. We sat in our old places, with the winter light at the window just as it had been when I was a child.

The castaways were still ensnared, still waiting to be saved. In one episode, Mr. Howell lost $3 million to Gilligan, betting over a makeshift putting green. I discovered I could still remember the lines. But now I understood one of the jokes for the first time. "I'm having trouble adjusting to this oyster shell putter," Mr. Howell said. Lovey replied, "Why, of course, it's because there's no *r* in the month." Watching a typical exchange between Gilligan and the Skipper in their skimpy bamboo hut, I enjoyed the Skipper's exaggerated mugging, the good-natured, slapstick humor. Why hadn't I seen this, in all those years?

I asked my mother whether she thought *Gilligan* was funny. Through all those years she'd caught the show from a distance, too busy, or unwilling, to sit with us for hours.

She laid down her paring knife. She was not watching the TV but looking through her spectacles at some memory I couldn't see. "Yes," she said.

"Why is it funny to you?"

"The show is funny because the characters were in an absurd situation," she replied. "They were unable to change with their environment."

"What is the difference between something funny and something sad?"

She did not answer. For a moment I felt that I had been transported to those years when my parents did not know if they would

THE MARY TYLER MOORE SHOW

Nora Ephron

I came late to *The Mary Tyler Moore Show*. I started watching it in 1973, and since you may have forgotten what things were like in 1973, let me refresh your memory: Mary had a much smaller apartment than the one she later moved to and the kitchen was on the left; Lou Grant was still married but fooling around; Ted Baxter was single; Phyllis lived downstairs with Lars; and Rhoda, recently having become thin and beautiful, was still making fat-and-funny-looking jokes. (I really missed Rhoda when she left. I thought she made a terrible mistake leaving Minneapolis and moving to New York for her own series and that big dumb husband CBS made her marry and then divorce.) Anyway, I started watching in 1973, in April, right after my first marriage broke up. It was a lovely time, not at all like the first time I was single, when there was nothing to watch on television on Saturday nights but *I Dream of Jeannie*. I actually used to watch it, too. Every week. In those days, I was somewhat more idiotic than

I am now about things like Saturday night and New Year's Eve. This is beginning to sound like an old Clearasil ad, and I don't mean to be doing that; all I want to say, without being too mushy about it, is that it meant a lot to me the second time I was single and home alone on Saturday night to discover that Mary Tyler Moore was home, too.

It has been pointed out on countless occasions that *The Mary Tyler Moore Show* was the first modern situation comedy in which the female star was not only not married but not engaged—but the important thing was that Mary Richards didn't even seem to care. There she was, turning the world on with her smile in the opening montage of the show, walking along with a bagful of groceries in her arms, and you could tell that she was on her way home to cook herself dinner for one. Calf's liver, I always thought. And maybe, after dinner, Georgette would stop by to say that Ted was very depressed. Or Lou would drop in with Murray. Or Phyllis would arrive from *her* series in San Francisco, which was an even bigger mistake than Rhoda's. You never could tell. But you could be pretty sure that there wouldn't be any strangers stopping in, because Mary Richards was usually Between Men. In fact, she was Between Men for entire seasons at a time. One year, there was a corny, slightly cross-eyed man in the construction business, a kind of male Rhoda, and it looked very serious between him and Mary—so serious that I considered writing a letter in protest, since he simply was not good enough for her—but he lasted only a couple of shows. And then he was gone. Really gone. Nobody ever asked about him afterward.

Mary never mentioned him. He just disappeared. And life went on, with Lou and Murray and Ted and Georgette and Sue Ann and Mary. Life went on, which was what the show was about. And then, after seven successful years on the air, *The Mary Tyler Moore Show* retired itself. Lou Grant returned the following year with his own series, though, like Rhoda and Phyllis, he didn't have the good sense to stay in Minneapolis where he belonged, either. But none of that takes away from my wanting to salute one of the best television shows in the history of the medium. Once, on the show on which Chuckles the clown was accidentally killed by a circus elephant, the subject got around to funerals, and Mary was asked what kind she wanted. "I just don't want an organ playing sad music," she said. Okay, Mary. I'll keep it short and sweet. Thanks. You made it possible for millions of Americans to stay home on Saturday night and not feel they were missing anything. For that alone I loved you.

INFOMERCIALS

Stephen McCauley

At age thirty-three, your life had gone from bad to worse, and worst of all by far, you had only yourself to blame. You'd made a lot of bad decisions in the areas of fidelity, honesty, and integrity. There had been, for example, a brief episode with your lover's best friend. There had been, for another example, a brief episode with your lover's best friend's lover. There had been a business trip that had nothing to do with business, a rented office you'd equipped with a sofa but no desk. And so on, in this general vein.

You had no explanations for your behavior and neither did your psychiatrist, possibly because you hadn't told him about it. He was an imposing man whose air of moral probity you admired. You were afraid he would be outraged by your actions and banish you from his office or, worse still, excuse you, thereby diminishing his moral authority in your eyes.

Two wrongs never make a right, it's true, but five, six, seven wrongs, each gaudy enough to be committed by a soap opera villain, can create sufficient havoc to blur the question of ethics.

At least for a while.

Bad decisions, like bad debts and cream-based sauces, have a way of catching up with you, and one day, you found yourself banished not from your morally superior shrink's office, but from the house you'd bought with your lover. You packed a couple of suitcases and took up residence in a dark and cramped sublet apartment with a lot of dusty books. A lot of cat hair. A window that looked out to an airshaft. A kitchen that smelled of coffee and bacon. And, in the far corner of a surprisingly large closet, a small black-and-white television set.

For nearly fifteen years, you'd lived without a television. You'd given up regular viewing around the time you became a vegetarian. Which was around the time you began doing Transcendental Meditation. Which was around the time you confronted your sexual preferences. All of which, not coincidentally, was around the time you moved out from under the parental thumb. Back then, a thin line of political reasoning had connected, TV, TM, tofu, and so on, but a decade and a half later, the line had grown fuzzy; you'd forgotten your mantra ages ago and you occasionally ate chicken. Not watching TV had become a habit, not a statement. You didn't own a set, and purchasing one—like purchasing a three-piece suit or a new car—was something you just couldn't imagine yourself doing. Cable-ready? You preferred to be the kind of person who wasn't sure what that meant. You got your news from the radio, your entertainment from movies and mischief, and watched Big Cultural Events—the Academy Awards, the last few games of the World Series—at friends' houses.

But in your cramped sublet, this appliance with its blank face and its quaint rabbit ear antennae had nostalgic charm. You set it up on a desk across from your bed and kept it there, even though it reflected back to you an unflattering, fish-eye picture of your solitude. At three A.M. one sleepless night, staring at your distorted self, you decided to take the next step and turn it on. The set came to life slowly, gradually filling the dark, silent room with flickering blue light and the reassuring cacophony of human voices. When you'd adjusted the antennae and fine-tuned the reception, you saw an energetic man in a chef's costume and an enthusiastic young woman discussing the virtues of a handheld kitchen appliance. A little more than a foot high and shaped like a wand, the appliance seemed, miraculously, to do everything. Blend soups. Make peanut butter. Shave ice. Whip skimmed milk into a fat-free froth.

You had no particular interest in cooking and were vaguely repulsed by the bluish pallor of skimmed milk, but something about this television show (for surely it was going on much too long to be a mere advertisement) captured your attention like nothing else had in the weeks following your relocation. And what was the explanation for that? The kitchen set, after all, was badly designed and reeked of cheap production values; the energetic man spoke with the too-careful articulation of a sidewalk religious fanatic; the enthusiastic woman stared into the camera with the wide-eyed awe of a bad actress portraying Bernadette's first sighting of Mary at Lourdes. The audience applauded and cheered each culinary feat with the gusto of drunken soccer fans, and the dialogue comprised mainly the word *amazing,* uttered with mounting hysteria.

But what was bad about the show (and that was nearly everything) was so authentically, unapologetically, and aggressively bad, you couldn't look away. The question of what the man in the chef's outfit would do next with the appliance had you rapt.

"Amazing," you'd find yourself muttering under your breath.

This was your first exposure to the "infomercial," that unsubtle blend of advertisement and entertainment, a half hour of unabashed hucksterism, and by the time the end credits were rolling, you were a devoted fan of the genre. Obviously television had come a long, long way in the fifteen years since you'd lived with a set under your roof.

In the weeks that followed, you discovered that these seductive programs were common on the airwaves in the middle of the night and throughout the morning on Sunday—not the most sought-after time slots—although no TV guide foretold their coming. They appeared on-screen unannounced, the way an elusive lover might show up unannounced on your doorstep at midnight. You found yourself sitting by the television in eager anticipation. (Now? *Now?*) The variety of products they promoted ran the gamut from the practical (vegetable juicers) to the just plain bizarre (spray-on hair for the balding). In between these two extremes were a lot of inventive oddities. The machine that makes "apple pie" from bottled applesauce and a slice of bread. The haircutting tool you hook up to a vacuum cleaner. The storage bag system that reduces a closet full of blankets and pillows to a shriveled packet the size of a loaf of bread. Exercise contraptions of Rube Goldberg complexity. Best of all, you got thirty minutes of uninterrupted programming because these were the only shows on commercial television that had *no commercials*!

The virtues of the products were promoted with demonstrations so irrelevant, they bordered on lunacy. In your favorite, feathers and cotton batting were lit on fire to prove that ordinary pillows don't keep a sleeping head as cool as ones filled with inflammable buckwheat husks. (Oh, okay.)

And still, you found yourself mesmerized by the satisfying conclusion of the demonstrations, no matter how irrelevant, and your pulse raced when the screen filled with the legend *The following program is a paid advertisement.* (Now!) You had an unlimited capacity to watch the same pitches over and over, some more than a dozen times, eagerly anticipating the flaming feathers, the shriveling pillows, the disappearing bald spots, and the fat-free foam. The unabashed awfulness filled you with joy, and sometimes, after viewing several in a row, an inexplicable, uncharacteristic optimism. There were performers who appeared in several infomercials, superstars of the medium: a cheerful, emaciated woman with pop eyes and unflagging enthusiasm for . . . everything, from carrot juice and dried fruit strips to acrylic mops; a sturdy, graying man with an air of well-deserved intellectual superiority—he, after all, had invented several of these wonders! They became celebrities in your eyes, vastly more engaging than the pretty movie stars featured on the covers of *Vanity Fair*. Their acting style transcended easy categories; somewhere between Grand Guignol and surrealist tableau vivant, it achieved a level of originality and theatrical absurdity that was unmatched elsewhere on the airwaves.

As did the programs themselves. It was easy to mock them, to laugh at them from the safe haven of ironic distance and the reassuring certainty that you were appreciating them as Not Quite Camp. But in the privacy of your solitary sublet, you began to question your motives. Once, twice, three times for a good laugh. Fine. But more than a dozen viewings? Was it possible that what you were experiencing when you watched these half-hour dramas with their obsequious hucksters and their horrid staging, their appalling actors and implausible studio audiences, was honest-to-God catharsis?

"Perhaps we should examine the themes," your psychiatrist suggested. (You'd been forced to tell him about your mistakes [some of them] and their consequences, but only because you couldn't think of another way to describe your discovery of infomercials and your compulsive viewing of them.)

Themes? In paid commercial programming? One looks for themes in literature and psychoanalysis. In Art. The idea of investigating the deeper meaning of advertising seemed crazy. And yet, that night, at one A.M., you begin to watch with more attention, looking for a connection between the vegetable juicer and the spray-on hair, the mop and the pizza-maker. A common thread.

You saw the historical context. These men and women with their explosive enthusiasm and adept handling of their goods were the direct descendants of snake-oil salesmen, hawking their miracle cures and beauty treatments from the back of a wagon. One part carnival barker, one part Elmer Gantry, all adapted for the attention-deficit demands of the television audience—the gullible children, the harried housewives, the lonely people in dusty sublet apartments.

As you were watching bread made into piecrust with Christlike speed for the fourteenth time, it hit you. How had you not seen it before? These were no mere product pitches; all of these shows were carefully crafted narratives of transformation. A problem is defined, a solution is offered, a change is instituted. The bald spot is made hairy, the embarrassingly hairy spot is depilated smooth, the vegetable is turned into liquid or into a dehydrated chew.

In the wake of this alchemy, whole lives were transformed. "It changed my life." "I became more confident." "It saved our marriage." "I got a promotion." "I'm so thankful." "I'm so happy."

Even a mop could alter a life: "I feel like a different person."

Amazing!

The infomercials were hawking dehydrators and detergents, roasters and grills, fishing rods and inflatable beds, but above all they were selling hope. They were hawking the idea that any problem could be solved with the mere flick of a switch and any life could be made much, much better.

You in your lonely sublet hadn't gone so far as to purchase the buckwheat pillow or the haircutting vacuum-cleaner attachment, but you were lapping up the hope.

"It's a place to start," your psychiatrist said.

Outside of the cozy, cheaply furnished world of infomercials, change takes time. It's easier to inflate a bed and deflate a pillow than it is to break old patterns and take responsibility for your actions, but with enough determination, optimism, and carrot juice, it can be done. You couldn't correct the mistakes of the past, but you could vow you wouldn't make them again. You could own up to your errors and offer apologies. When the urge to take a step backward and make bad decisions struck, you could turn on the television and wait for a reminder that there was a better way.

Bit by bit, you moved on. You bid good-bye to the betrayed lover and the untidy network of best friends and the office that wasn't much suited for work and the cramped sublet apartment. You found a place to live that had more light and no cat hair. The books on the shelves were no less dusty, but now they were your own. You bought a cable-ready TV, and then a three-piece suit, and then a new car. You could say, "I feel like a different person," without much irony at all. Amazing.

In time, the heyday of the infomercial seemed to pass. Or maybe, being less in the market for manufactured hope, you were simply less aware of the presence of half-hour commercials for the same.

Except:

One more recent end-of-summer day, you found yourself indoors on a bright, hot morning watching the television real-time images of a tragedy so vast and horrifying in its implications, you were repeatedly sick. The images seemed to signal, even in their earliest moments, an inevitable turning point in the life of the country—culturally, politically, spiritually. You, along with the rest of the world, watched in silence for hours and hours. Until: You

early 1970s, when we got that first glimpse of a bizarre British phenomenon called *Monty Python's Flying Circus* on PBS, late at night (even after *Don Kirschner's Rock Concert*). For a bleary-eyed fourteen-year-old sitting in some suburban couple's idea of the fully realized American dream den, "Spam, eggs, sausage, and Spam" seemed like a personal message—an acknowledgment that life's menu wasn't offering any real alternatives. It was all Spam.

A few years later, those of us who responded so intensely to Monty Python had found one another, and learned we were part of what is called a "cult following." We all bought Monty Python records and tickets for their New York appearances, and helped turn them into a national phenomenon.

The more obscure the media reference, the more profound the bond between those of us who shared it. Although it's always tremendously gratifying to find someone else who remembers some phantom television event from my past, it's also oddly disappointing. It feels as if the acknowledgment somehow confirms what may have been a television fantasy into a fact. No—I wasn't dreaming that television moment. It really happened, and other people experienced it, too. The same way I did.

Maybe that's why college, for me, was mainly an opportunity to compare and contrast television moments with people from other parts of the country. I remember there was one particular show I really wanted to know if anyone else had experienced: a short black-and-white film called *The Cube*.

The movie aired as part of a Sunday-morning Christian drama series in the late 1960s. In it, a man discovers himself trapped in a small, room-sized cube. The walls are white squares. He is visited by several people, including a small child on a tricycle who taunts him. When he punches his fist through the wall, a repairman enters with a new piece of wall that fits in the jagged hole perfectly.

I watched it with my father, and remember being disturbed. It depicted the archetypal alone-with-the-tube situation, for this man looked like he was literally inside the TV set. The whole piece was shot as if the cube in which he was trapped was the very box of the television. It seemed to mirror my entire childhood.

My dad didn't seem similarly affected. I once asked him about it, and he had no memory of it at all. Who knows if he was even watching? It was Sunday morning. He was probably just sitting there asleep on the couch while his eight-year-old son got traumatized. Or maybe I was the one who had been asleep—dreaming of this strange cube while my dad sat there watching something as innocuous as *F-Troop*.

The program was so unsettling—nestled in my memory so precariously between fact and dream—that I didn't bring it up to any of my college friends. Each time one of those TV conversations came around to "Did you see this?" or "Did you see that?" I always held my tongue. What was I afraid of?

It was a few years after graduation, while pretending to be successful writers and drinking six-dollar whiskey at Elaine's, that a buddy of mine, Walter, and I happened to revisit the topic of television and those oddly personal media milestones. Walt slid his shot glass away, as if to clear the space between us, and said, "Look, I don't know for sure the details, or if this is even real or not, but there was a program I saw when I was a kid. . . ."

Yes, he, too, had seen the show. It *must* have been real. Between the two of us, we pieced together more details. More confident of the reality of our shared experience, we began to question our other friends. A few weeks later, we found a third person who had seen the same program—and likewise, felt his worldview had somehow been skewed by this single, isolated, television experience.

The Web hadn't been invented yet, but the Internet did have

a few early bulletin boards. We posted a query about *The Cube*, and our sense of urgency at finding out anything we could about the film, and got half a dozen responses. We had found our *Cube* community, and a television event that had receded so far that none of us knew if it had been real or a dream but was now a reality and a basis for connection.

Thanks to the near-infinite recesses of the cable box, TV is now a landscape to be explored in this fashion. And I suppose the Internet is really just the place to share what we've found.

But it's those first moments of discovery—those jaw-dropping moments when you happen upon, say, *Iron Chef* in Japanese, the *Robyn Byrd* stripper show, or the original *Colonel Bleep* cartoons— that make you feel as if you are the only one in the universe who is watching. Or at least the only one who is watching it in that way.

I had such a moment in 1991, shortly after returning to New York from a rather meaningless eight-year stint in Los Angeles writing film scripts that were optioned but never made. I was feeling truly alone, again, for the first time since childhood, and spent many evenings roaming the upper reaches of the cable box. That's when I first came upon an old black-and-white science fiction serial, *Radar Men from the Moon.* At the bottom of the screen, as a line in a Looney Tunes cartoon, was the black silhouette of a man sitting in a row of movie theater seats. On either side of him sat what appeared to be a gumball machine and a lacrosse stick. All three of them had voices, and made sarcastic comments about the painfully horrid film. I took it for some strange "public access" experiment, and moved on.

But I ran into them again and again over the coming months, and eventually learned that these three characters—a human and two robots—were part of a cult TV show out of Minneapolis called *Mystery Science Theater 3000.* The premise was, basically, that a young inventor had been launched into space by his evil boss. He would now be forced to watch terrible sci-fi B-movies, like *Horrors of Spider Island,* on his spaceship for the rest of his life. To keep himself from going crazy, he built two robots to keep him company while he watched the movies.

The show perfectly recapitulated my own situation. I, too, was trapped—in a New York City high-rise studio on a cold winter night. Now, instead of watching bad television alone, I had some electronic companionship—just like the guy stuck in the space station. Technology would be my friend.

So in each episode, this character sits and watches movies like *Horrors of Spider Island, The Deadly Mantis,* or *Santa Claus Conquers the Martians,* while he and his robots make wry commentary. Their comments elevate the worst backwater of television into a fresh, almost live event. A media recycling plant. I was no longer merely watching television, but watching *the* television. The three characters at the edge of the screen served as a bracketing devise—an almost Brechtian alienation effect—commenting on the action, and giving me permission to be entertained by a movie that I knew full well was basically crap.

What's more, the jokes these three people—well, one person and two robots—told were very targeted. These didn't seem like jokes everyone in the world would understand. It required a pretty good knowledge of the science fiction universe, of 1970s television, even of physics. It was a nerd's-eye view of the mediascape.

That's why I was so surprised when, on one episode, they took a moment to invent an "Andrew Lloyd Weber Grill" on which the composer's overwrought show scores could be burned. They continued to make sly references to *Evita* and *Cats,* and even *Joseph and the Amazing Technicolor Dreamcoat.* Having spent a childhood doing summer stock musicals, I knew every reference. But how were the science fiction people supposed to know all that? Was I the only one who got those jokes, or were many science fiction nerds also educated in the sad decline of the Broadway musical?

In another episode, in the movie the trio are watching, an arm swings through the frame. One of the robots begins humming a tune that I immediately recognize as the theme from *My Three Sons*. Of course, I realize—the opening credits of the old sixties TV show consisted of a cartoon arm swinging back and forth through the frame. Did everyone else get that, or just a few people? Or just me? Might they have told a joke for which I was the sole comprehending audience?

Of course not. Well, at least probably not. But that's not as important as the fact that they re-created the *Cube* sensation. That lonely, late-night, Monty Python recognition. And they were using obscure media references to do it! This entire program was a litany of private media moments—spirits from television's past, called back into the present. Thousands of childhood sensations, revived and confirmed.

That's why a show like *Mystery Science Theater 3000—MST3K* to its fans—is so meticulously indexed and cataloged by its many archivists online. It's as if to prevent these insights—these acknowledgments and confirmations—from slipping back into the ether again. To enjoy *MST3K* is to get the media references. This is not a show based in conflict and resolution; there is no plot. The entertainment value is in making the connections. Between oneself and the tube and, eventually on-line, with others who experienced those media moments too.

The same television that isolated us for decades was now providing us with the very beginnings of a strategy through which to relate to one another, once again. True, we had all spent childhoods alone with the television—but now we could talk about those experiences, and realize we had all gone through them, together. That's why people enjoy talking about shows as bad as *Gilligan's Island* and *The Brady Bunch*. Because we were all experiencing something more than the programs themselves. We were all thinking about whether Greg smoked pot in that special bedroom they built for him. Or whether the Professor ever got it on with Mary Ann.

For me, this nearly obsessively self-conscious viewing style almost always happened during science fiction programs. Maybe it was the fact that TV is a technology, too, so that a program about technology viewed through a technology will always tend to take on an allegorical quality. Whatever the reason, the worlds depicted on sci-fi shows were not alien places at all—they were my home.

Lost in Space was the formative example, for sure. Because I was Will Robinson. Sure, I dreamed I was Will and on alien planets and all, but that's not the most intense experience I had of being the young boy lost in space with his family, robot, and evil, queer psychologist.

Growing up on the suburban frontier of Larchmont, New York, felt as much like space travel as anything the Robinsons were going through. Will was a boy alone. The only potential friends he had were aliens who happened to knock on the spaceship door—creatures his parents wouldn't or couldn't trust, no matter how good they might be as playmates.

This was life in the suburban landscape as well, where appearances were more important than genuine connections. The maintenance of one's patch of shrubbery or driveway tar took on greater meaning than any human relationships. Each family lived alone in its own aluminum-clad fortress, coming outside only long enough to drive the kids to school, pick up the groceries, and compliment the neighbor on her good looks before retreating to the telephone and gossiping about the possibility that she'd gotten a face-lift.

We kids always wondered what was the big deal? Why were the children next door on the left okay to play with, while the ones on the right were "no good"? Like Will Robinson (or, to be fair, his sister Penny), why were we kids the only ones who knew enough to look beneath the surface, and to realize that the "Gold-faced" alien was not to be trusted, while the little ugly lizard-man had a heart of gold? What sort of value system had our parents adopted? And would we, one day, share it?

The only ones Will Robinson really had to talk to were his mechanical pal, Robot, and the strange and evil Dr. Smith. Robot was always the more interesting one to me, because he was like the TV set. Yes, everything he said was programmed, but it all seemed so much more real and relevant than anything human beings wanted to say. And, like the TV, he was always there—always aiming to please. His illuminated red breastplate, flashing while he spoke, became the screen within my own television screen. A window into the heart and soul of the TV set.

Maybe that's why the moment I'll always remember best—the one that led me to begin my carefully documented set of synopses and sketches for every single episode—was the one where Robot is in an accident that causes him to grow several hundred times his normal size. Will, and a reluctant Dr. Smith, must travel inside Robot to repair him. They confront Robot's various antibodies and wind through his many passages, until they at last encounter his heart, where they make the needed repairs.

Did my television set have a heart as well?

Of course, playing to Will from the opposite end of civilization's spectrum was Dr. Smith. We all figured he was played by an old, gay Shakespearean actor (Jonathan Harris was actually a happily married, Jewish ex-pharmacist from the Bronx), but this mythology had more to do with Smith's role in the show, and the way he declined in stature from a conniving and dangerous villain into an effete, bumbling, and selfish clown.

Smith was everything Robot was not: disloyal, self-serving, emotionally driven, and sexually suspect. Just why was this guy spending so much time with a boy on the brink of puberty? When he wasn't attempting to use the boy as a pawn in one of his plots, Smith was grabbing him from behind and pressing him against his chest as protection from whichever monster he had irritated this time.

Smith represented the past—the world of literature, the Cold War (he started out as a Russian agent), Freudian psychology, and profit-minded trickery. Robot, on the other hand, came from a world delightfully unencumbered by these legacies. Surely his memory banks held the facts of the Nazis and the atomic wars, but his heart bore none of the scars. Like those of us watching the show, he was an innocent—both smarter than his keepers and free of their prejudices and values. Dr. Smith would regularly risk the lives of his crew members for the chance to steal a pile of gems. What good would a chest filled with diamonds do him in outer space, anyway?

Not to mention the adults' never-ending obsession with getting back home. Like it was really better back there or then? The one time Will succeeds in getting home (using an alien device), no one believes he is really from the Robinson family at all! Like the many young nerds watching the program, he is as much an alien on earth as he is anywhere else.

Best to stick with Robot. Like the television itself, he is the ideal companion.

Science fiction programs were not a way to learn about space or aliens, but an encounter with the virtual soul of television. Only shows that imbue technology with heart, or the TV screen with the ability to see into worlds unavailable to us any other way, are capable of enacting this transubstantiation of cathode ray into social nourishment.

Mystery Science Theater 3000 was a TV lover's show. Unlike the reruns on *Nick at Nite,* which give its viewers the thrill of pure, ignorant nostalgia under the false guise of irony, *MST3K* reunites us with the wise naïveté of genuine, mindful, technological engagement. It is a way to watch with awareness, to reconnect the dots, and to return to the lucid dream of television with the multiple awareness of a quantum physicist.

Most of all, it serves as a touchstone. It's a repository of those TV moments too special to risk sharing with others—those observations we all made, but never felt confident enough to find out if everyone else had made, too.

And it proves that those of us who seemed to have nothing to comfort us in our childhood other than the TV set were never truly alone.

PART FOUR

GREAT ESCAPES

A LIFE of DANGER

April Bernard

I: From Memory

The television dwelt in the basement, in what a realtor would have called a "rec" room, but we called the "play" room, and with the cement only a quarter-inch away, the brown-and-yellow-spatter floor tiles always felt cold. The mysteries of television land filled that chilly room, in big double-shadowed black-and-white images, excluding NBC. We did not "receive" NBC. I have never seen even five minutes of *Bonanza*, and I have shocked friends with this revelation, much as if I had told them I'd never read *King Lear*. On the other hand, there were all the Saturday nights that I joined my parents to watch Patrick McGoohan in the British import series *Danger Man*, retitled in the United States, with a new theme song by Johnny Rivers, as *Secret Agent*.

My *first* TV romance was with Mighty Mouse. It is still unclear whether I desired him or wanted to *be* him, but it was probably both. Other images of male desirability arrived as Sugar

Foot, the Constitution-totin' lawyer of the Wild West, and a curly-haired dance-show host named Lloyd Thaxton, whose local (out of Albany, New York) after-school show featured the Freddy, the Frug, and the Lloyd Thaxton Hop. Perhaps because of its basement locale, perhaps because my older brother and sister were so bossy that I deliberately chose to watch shows they couldn't stand—in any case, from the first, the TV was solitary sex-dream land for me. Huddled under the old chenille bedspread that covered the battered playroom couch, I learned all sorts of bizarre falsehoods, distortions, and occasional truths about men and women and desire. Of course, this is so for most everyone. We have bent those impressions to our own needs, however; I dare say you've seen *The Dick Van Dyke Show,* but you might be surprised to know that I was so mortified by Dick's clowning that I would hide my face or run from the room until the laughter died down. Depending on that week's plot, Dick's character, Rob Petrie, under the influence of alcohol or a sedative, or sleepwalking, would go all rubbery and tilt and sway as he crossed the room, always, it seemed, finally falling down in a dismaying pretzel somersault that exaggerated the indignity. Or he would get an idea that everyone, especially his wife, would ridicule, but he would pursue it—a fear that he was losing his mind, or was about to die from a dread disease, or was being one-upped by the neighbors—until it created havoc and widespread embarrassment. He would decide to stand up to the boss, and then, in the crisis moment, cringe, clear his throat, and change his mind. The show was funny to me, but though I wanted to love Rob Petrie, he was always letting me down. I experienced his physical looseness, his cowardice, and his willingness to be silly to win a point—that is, his comic persona— as a prompt of sexual shame.

We lived in the northwest corner of Massachusetts, where if we were lucky—and the wind was right, and the antenna on straight—we could get one station out of Albany and another out of Springfield. We were surrounded by farm country, though we were neither quite rural village nor suburban tract, but something in between. Our house was in a small "development" built on old farm-wood lot land sometime in the 1930s—cute, all-different houses on streets that formed a clumsily bisected circle, like a pattern in the snow for Duck, Duck, Goose. Most of the old shade trees had been left intact. The fathers were teachers or doctors or small businessmen; or, as was the case with my father, research scientists with a brief daily commute to one of the nearby cities. The mothers were housewives—and if some of them, like my mother, had once had real careers as scientists or librarians (she'd been both), it was not a subject for discussion. I wanted, most of the time, to be a boy. But I was too small and uncoordinated to be much of a tomboy, so instead I studied the TV world of men and women, because I was reasonably sure that though I would be a woman, I would have to be one of *those* women—the ones with power, the ones men looked at nervously and dared great things for. I adored *The Secret Storm* and *The Edge of Night,* soap operas that featured many divas.

Meanwhile my parents were busy resembling, as cheerfully as they could under the strain of four children and the boondocks, sophisticates. My father was boyish, a joker; my mother was often told she looked like Audrey Hepburn—and they had a kind of low-key glamour that is astonishing to my sight when I see old photos. They look quite a lot, in fact, like the Petries— who looked, it has often been remarked, quite a lot like the Kennedys—and though we didn't live in New Rochelle, not by a long shot, my father's business did take him to New York a few times a year. When my mother went with him, they returned to tell stories of Broadway shows and nightclubs and, once, to give us children a demonstration of the twist. My mother was the very first person I ever saw (except on TV) in a pair of bell-bottoms—fuchsia velvet, big-belted, hip-huggers with swirling bell bottoms—and a cream lace-covered faux-sheer blouse to go with it, straight from I. Magnin in 1966.

In any case, I cannot doubt that my shame at the antics of Dick Van Dyke's Rob Petrie character had to do with a conflation of him with my father—nor can I doubt that the breeze of sexuality that accompanied my parents whenever they returned from a trip lodged in my mind, for all eternity, the conviction that New York City was the only place worth living. And then, as my older brother and sister lost all interest in my parents and my younger brother was still the baby, I somehow got myself caught up in their chief courtship ritual, Saturday-night dinner.

They fed us early. After the baby was asleep, they sat down in front of the television with martinis—Gibsons—and potato chips with cream-cheese-and-chive dip; then my father would grill steak, and, with French bread from the new classy bakery in town and Boston lettuce salad with vinaigrette dressing, they would dine. Somehow we received *Secret Agent* on one of our two channels, and somehow I caught the fever and was allowed to sit with them in the basement to watch. I had never heard of spies, really, nor had I yet heard of James Bond—and would not have grasped the kind of burlesque Ian Fleming and those movies offered in any case. Irony of that sort was lost on me. I took *Secret Agent* straight, and I took it quietly, with awe, as I ate the pickled onions out of the martinis.

Unlike Rob Petrie, the Secret Agent never made goofy gestures or kowtowed to a boss or tried to please a wife. He was a sleek, snide loner, who only collapsed, and that gracefully, when felled by a judo chop or a mickey in his drink. He was lethally charming; jaunty electric organ music accompanied his journeys; women with hair shaped into tall cones or bubbles, wearing geometric dresses up to here, all desired him or wanted to kill him. It was the same thing. And I wanted him, and I wanted to be him, and that was the same thing, too.

A few other shards come to me in memory: a tape recorder the size of a pack of cards, discovered in a potted palm; a bald bad guy with two thugs coming in through the French doors; champagne glasses snatched from a thousand dancing trays at a vast party under chandeliers; a bitter sarcastic taunt from the Agent to the thug just before the thug levels him with a blow to the gut; words, many words, urgent, whispered by a woman to a man, almost overheard through an open window.

II: *DANGER MAN* IN 2004

They are all on DVD now, those old episodes, and I have swum for weeks in all fifty-plus hours of nonstop Patrick McGoohan—his secret-agent name is John Drake, one of many details I had forgotten. At first I found myself at a stance of great detachment from the old shows, pondering concepts like Cold War Subversion and Late Capitalism, relishing the clean lines of black and white, admiring the swinging-sixties clothes. Some episodes seem gauche now; some are exciting; all are amusing. But over time I slid into the world of *Danger Man* on its own terms, grateful for the innocence of those years, and happy to acknowledge that its subject matter remains, for me, essentially sexual, impossibly adult, and deeply romantic. My reeducation can be summed up as follows.

Things I Learned from **Secret Agent/Danger Man** *That Turn Out Not to Be True:*
- Bad guys make the fatal mistake of gloating before they pull the trigger.

- African leaders are grateful for British Intelligence interference in their affairs.
- It's charming to be insulted by a handsome man.
- A jet touching down on a foreign airfield makes an exciting beginning to a TV show.
- Tiny-brimmed fedoras are fashionable.
- Women with long, loose hair are good; women with updos are bad.
- One unarmed man, employing various martial arts, can take out five armed men.

Things That Turn Out to Be True After All:
- Sexy men move like cats.
- Guns are in bad taste.
- No one likes to be fooled.
- Goddesses are always half an hour late.
- Keep your back to the light.
- Check the exits.
- Kiss but don't tell.

PRIME TIMES

Michael Gorra

This is the shot I remember. A middle-aged man in a black topcoat and bowler hat stands in the twilight against a long, low arcade. A dog barks in the distance—the only sound here—and the man turns and walks on, the camera following as he steps into something like symmetry, as we see that this arcade is matched by another one, far away across a smooth piece of lawn. But however grand, they are now revealed as nothing more than outbuildings, two arms, really, while the body that links them is a tawny-stoned country house, with a high central window that gives back a coppery light. The man stops before the house, looks up, and the camera cuts to his face, to raised eyebrows and a half-smile. Then he heads toward the side door, caught in the embrace of an ordered world that could all be his.

Or at least his after a fashion. The man is named Hudson, and he is, as he says, the butler to "Mr. Richard Bellamy and the late Lady Marjorie Bellamy," the Lady Marjorie having gone down a few episodes before on the *Titanic*. And the scene I've described comes from the second American season of *Upstairs, Downstairs*, which ran on PBS's *Masterpiece Theatre* in the fall of 1974. Here's the story: "Captain James," the Bellamys' always disappointing son, has gone for a weekend's shooting in the country, taking Hudson as his valet and loader. Upstairs at Somerby Park, James flirts with a titled beauty but doesn't finally propose, in part because of a talk with a Jewish financier whom the other houseguests all snub. While downstairs, having first made it clear that he is *not* a valet, Hudson manages to save a luncheon party from the senile and alcoholic incompetence of the place's own butler. Soon the most discreet of job offers is laid before him, a job that includes running not just this house, but ones in London and Scotland as well. Standing in the half-light before Somerby's great central block, Hudson is tempted indeed, a temptation inseparable from his knowledge that he would be up to the challenge.

Of course, he decides in the end to stay on with the Bellamys in Eaton Place. And watching it today on video, I see all sorts of things I didn't, or couldn't, have known when I first saw this episode. I can give the house an approximate date, around 1730, and I can recognize that it was centrally planned, a place that would have gone up all at once rather than growing slowly through the years. I know that the very name of Somerby's housekeeper—Mrs. Kenton—was picked up fifteen years later by a British novelist whom no one in this late-Edwardian world could have imagined: Kazuo Ishiguro uses it for the housekeeper in *The Remains of the Day*. I know, too, now, that the director's decision to set the scene at dusk is a cliché, history breathing down the characters' collective neck. And while I can't claim that watching *Upstairs, Downstairs* helped me learn any of this, still there does seem to be a connection. I was a senior in high school and impatient to leave home for college when I saw that episode, and the two things got themselves confused in my mind. I didn't exactly see my future in butlering, but however strange it now seems, I drew an analogy between the worlds opening out to Hudson, and to me. We both wanted a wider experience.

I watched *Masterpiece Theatre* on and off for more than twenty years; mostly off and unsatisfied with what I did see for many of them, but entirely on and enthralled at the start. I missed the historical shows with which the program began at the start of the seventies, things like *The First Churchills* and *Elizabeth R.* The early twentieth century in general and *Upstairs, Downstairs* in particular was where I came in, and as with most of the television that matters, my viewing is in memory inseparable from the company and the time and the place. I watched with my mother, the two of us sitting on the couch together, Sunday evenings at nine, in the family room of our house in eastern Connecticut, up half a flight from what must be called a "breakfast nook," with the television sitting on the wide hearth of a fireplace we almost never used. My younger brother would have been upstairs, watching something of his own on the black-and-white set in his room; my father would have been asleep, preparing for a workday that would start around midnight.

Aside from an occasional illicit Heineken, the show stands as the first foreign product that I used precisely because it was foreign. My parents drove American cars, as nearly as I can remember we wore anonymous undesigned American clothing, and we barely ever ate Brie. I had never seen a movie with subtitles, Penguin hadn't yet fully cracked the American market, and nobody I knew had spent more than the length of a package tour in Europe unless the army had sent them there. So for the moment, and until college—or rather, "life"—began, the show itself became the focus of my own invidious cultural longings. And two of its features in particular seemed to underwrite those longings. First, it depended on adaptations, and second, the actors had accents.

Even *Upstairs, Downstairs*, which had no direct literary model, still seemed like an adaptation, a spin-off from some unwritten original. That was a selling point, because for my mother and in consequence for me, it was an article of faith that books were always better than TV or even movies. To watch the show you at least had to be interested in books, and books had always been a kind of secret knowledge between us, even if in my own reading I couldn't yet discriminate between *A Farewell to Arms* and *The Guns of Navarone.* TV at that time was supposed to be a democratic medium, but PBS, which aired *Masterpiece Theatre,* was the original niche audience, and I liked the fact that nobody else I knew seemed to watch it, not my mother's friends, and certainly not any of the boys with whom I played football. Maybe the girl down the street did. She was already losing herself in books with titles I didn't recognize, *Middlemarch* or *Bleak House,* thick old things it wouldn't have occurred to me to open.

As for the accents, while I didn't want one myself, I at least wanted to know people who did have them. If you're charitable, you could say that I simply wanted a larger world than my hometown could offer. If you're not—well, I've said it all to myself before. I was a New Englander all hot for an old England, a Jamesian before I'd read a word of him, and prone to what he calls a "superstitious overvaluation" of an abroad I'd never seen and knew nothing about; overvalued, indeed, precisely because I *didn't* know anything about it. Would I have been so fascinated if *Masterpiece Theatre* had put on *Ethan Frome* or *A Hazard of New Fortunes* or even *The Great Gatsby,* if the scripts and the acting had been as good but the accents American? Don't be silly. I could no more have appreciated them than I did the originality of *The Rockford Files.* I preferred the derivative and the far away, I wanted London, not New York, and all through that last year at home, I made my weekly devotion—sometimes I even watched the midweek repeat!—as if attending to that video equivalent of Mantovani might help me get to the real thing at last.

Perhaps indeed it did. It's easy enough these days to find a video of most shows from that period, but they don't give you its full flavor. They have the credit shots and theme music for that particular production—a light waltz for *Upstairs, Downstairs,* a syncopated dissonance for adaptations of Dorothy Sayers, which later became the theme for *Mystery!* But they don't provide the framing material for *Masterpiece Theatre* itself: the trumpet call that to my dismay turned out to be French; the overstuffed drawing room, with its framed stills from various programs, family photographs that got added to year by year as the backlist grew; and above all the aged and ageless face of its host. One night Alastair Cooke came on after an episode of Sayers's *Murder Must Advertise,* with Ian Carmichael as a plumply unconvincing Lord Peter, an episode that featured costume parties and cocaine and false young voices. "Dorothy Sayers was not," he said as he opened the book in his lap, "the only writer to describe the world of London parties in the twenties," and then he began to read from Evelyn Waugh's *Vile Bodies.* I still remember the passage:

> *So they all got into taxicabs again and drove rather a long way to Miss Brown's house. She turned on the lights in a sombre dining-room and gave them glasses of whisky and soda. . . . Then Miles said he wanted something to eat, so they all went downstairs into a huge kitchen lined with every shape of pot and pan and found some eggs and some bacon and Miss Brown cooked them. Then they had some more whisky upstairs and Adam fell asleep again. Presently Vanburgh said, "D'you mind if I use the telephone? I must just send in the rest of my story to the paper."*

Vanburgh is a gossip columnist, and the story contains what none of the other guests realize: The site of this impromptu party is No. 10 Downing Street, and mousy little Miss Brown is the prime minister's daughter. The next morning there are cameras waiting in the street outside, and that afternoon the government falls.

Cooke must have read for five minutes or more, and by the time he finished my eyes were streaming with laughter. But who was Evelyn Waugh? "You know, I have that one," my mother said, and we went out to the book-lined hallway to find it, a cheap undersized Dell paperback that contained both *Vile Bodies* and *Black Mischief.* Two for one—as good a deal as the science fiction I spent most of my time on. And by the next Sunday I had read them both, cackling madly page after page, even though I wasn't sure what to make of their endings, when all the life seemed to drain out of the jokes but you kept on laughing anyway.

Waugh died in 1966. When I discovered him his reputation had gone into the usual postmortem ditch, though I did come upon another paperback double, *Decline and Fall* packaged with *A Handful of Dust*; the Little, Brown uniform edition I still use began to appear in 1977. By that time he had started to claw his way out of the trough, even if it would be a few years before he turned up on PBS himself. *Brideshead Revisited* ran here in 1982, on *Great Performances* rather than *Masterpiece Theatre,* a distinction that seems even more meaningless now than it did then. I didn't watch it. I was in graduate school, my evenings were full, my rabbit-eared TV wouldn't pull it in—and there were other reasons, too. I had started a dissertation that included a chapter on Waugh himself, but however much I loved his comedy, I was also what the English call a cradle Catholic, and I loathed that particular book's convert snobbery (though not as much as I disliked its empurpled account of the Lady Julia's "narrow loins"). Yet more important was the fact that I had, by then, become a snob about the very kind of show that had brought me to Waugh—and even perhaps to graduate school—in the first place.

Middlebrow, bourgeois, escapist—*Brideshead Revisited* was indeed all that, as a novel at least, and those adjectives can stand, too, for the usual dismissal that *Masterpiece Theatre* itself received in its heyday. Costumes, accents, servants, the past, a safe past that couldn't hurt us, at least not over here. I loved all that, and if you push on most English teachers my age, they'll admit to having loved it, too, to having their own period of swooning Anglophilia in front of their parents' TV. Within a few years, however, I found myself sharing that criticism: thought *Poldark* a bore, resented the narrative short cuts in a 1980 *Pride and Prejudice,* and wished I'd never heard of H. E. Bates. So maybe *Masterpiece Theatre* did its work too well. By now I really did agree with my mother: Books *were* better than TV, at least this kind of TV. Yet along with my Faulkner and Waugh I was also putting in time with *Hill Street Blues* and even with *Dallas,* and knew that television itself did indeed have something to give me.

"Couldn't you write about something a bit, well, a bit more pop?" my wife said when I told her I was working on this piece. And there is indeed something embarrassing in writing about such a show. TV isn't supposed to be about restraint or judgment or taste, but that's what I learned on Sunday evenings at nine, and perhaps the real embarrassment lies in having to admit that that is in fact where I learned them. "Pop" is precisely what at seventeen I *didn't* want to be, and I suppose *Masterpiece Theatre* is something I had to get over before I could admit to enjoying *Cheers* or *The Dick Van Dyke Show,* before I could come to anything like a full appreciation of the American popular culture in which I'd grown up. But nothing else I watched then speaks so clearly to the person I wanted to become.

DREAMHOUSE

Virginia Heffernan

I wanted to see the Advent candles. I don't think Andrew cared, though a few years later he got so excited about Christmas he threw up. Our family had white candles from Rich's—stuck with wax to a doubled paper plate and ringed with fir twigs—and after I begged her to, my mother lit all four of them and set the plate on a black-and-white Zenith, our television set. We had just gotten home from church.

Davey and Goliath confused us. On Sundays Andrew and I had the run of the networks, but they were dry of cartoons. Instead, men who looked like Nixon but who might have been his prosecutors talked over our heads. We were both under five. *Davey and Goliath looked* like a normal kids' show, with pratfalls, light laughter, and dolls reeling around in stop-action animation, but it was also an offering from the Lutheran Church of America and therefore potentially an extension of Sunday school. According to current nostalgia websites, *Davey and Goliath*, which may soon be reprised, promoted tolerance, honesty, civic duty, and faith. Generally, Andrew and I conferred about whether to watch it, knowing sort of that whatever mischief of Davey's excited us in the beginning of the show would be condemned by the end, that Bible verses might be quoted, and that Davey would learn lessons, liberal but unusual religious teachings.

The Lutheran Church wasn't our church, and its understated presence on the show—Davey and Goliath were not only not mortal enemies but were boy-and-dog pals—seemed more intimidating than inviting. The religious motif was also very faint. This raised suspicions. At our church we knew when to be *en garde,* ignoring far-out teachers who forced mustard seeds on us or who speculated about the tendons in Jesus' hands. On *Davey and Goliath* we frequently couldn't tell what was going down at all. Still, Davey Hanson's face was round and cheerful, and his dog had a low, dopey voice. Andrew and I agreed, as we had in the past, that Davey and Goliath were better than the politicians and evangelists on other channels, who in turn seemed more boring, even, than no television at all.

The episode, I now know, was called "Doghouse Dreamhouse." In it, Davey learns that life is best when you don't have to lean on people and holler for help. It's a rough lesson. In one of the opening scenes, Mr. Hanson urges Davey, who doesn't believe he can do carpentry on his own, to make a new doghouse for Goliath by himself. "You'll be surprised what you can do," Mr. Hanson says. "I don't want to be surprised," says Davey.

We liked this one. Exchanges like that, in which a kid failed in a deadpan way to respond to adult encouragement, cracked us up. My father was at his office in town, finishing his work before we packed up and left for London, where we were about to spend a year. My mother was grading papers two rooms away. She had taught college before we were born; now she helped professors part-time. My mother found Mr. Rogers untrustworthy, and later she thought that *Three's Company* degraded women, but she was busy that day, and I don't know if she worried about whether what Andrew and I were watching was sacred or profane. Or preachy, which to her was often worse.

Davey and Goliath always opens with a shot of a cross in a red heart in a royal crest or a white flower, all set against something that resembles a coin. A primitive synthesizer plays a distorted version of a familiar hymn. Davey, on his knees in a red-and-white-checked shirt and brown pants, with neat, immobile brown hair, lights a rocket while big Goliath, the breed-less dog, stands by. Davey fires off the rocket from a spot behind a stone; it zooms up, spelling DAVEY AND GOLIATH in the air. Then the title drops down and re-forms the cross-heart-flower.

Andrew did not want to leave for London. He used to develop close alliances with objects, and he dreaded leaving his bed, his chairs, and his room. He liked to draw tableaus of superheroes and their adventures. Left-handed, he curled his arm around the top of a page and drew comics the Marvel way. But that must have been when he was older. He was only two on that day we watched "Doghouse Dreamhouse," and he may only have drawn nonsense shapes, but he was meticulous always. I was impulsive and I couldn't wait to get to London, of which I had no concept at all.

The episode begins with an electrical storm. Davey and Goliath watch it from Davey's room, with Goliath musing in a voice only Davey can hear about whether it's too wet for him to sleep outside. The question becomes moot when a lightning bolt shatters his doghouse. When the night lights up, you get a brief look at the skyline of Davey's town, a tidy, ethnically diverse town with very little crime. Goliath is bereft.

"Oh, come on, Goliath, you live in my house, too," Davey says.

"Sometimes I like a private house," Goliath says, and it sounds sinister, like a father explaining divorce to his children. I didn't like the idea of people needing privacy.

The doghouse is a shambles. Davey goes to see his father about collaborating on the rebuilding project. The Hansons' house is modern inside, with clean-lined tables and an elegant midcentury lamp, trimmed with rickrack, in what looked like actual size.

Nothing had jostled our TV, but one of the Advent candles burned unevenly, and it tilted on the plate. Sometime later it fell flat.

"When can we start, Dad?"

"Not now, Davey. You . . . We've built lots of things to-gether—scooters, Sally's dollhouse, chicken coops out at Grandpa's farm. I've taught you all the basics. Now let's see what you can do on your own." My own dad talked this way, so I fig-ured the show was realistic, the first term of evaluation I learned, and the only one Andrew and I had for a long time. Even now, when we e-mail about new movies, we guiltily revert to calling the ones we like "realistic."

Davey's father is called away on business, after a work-related long-distance phone call. Abandoned, Davey schemes to build the doghouse, but to do so halfheartedly, so shoddily that his fa-ther will have to agree that he can't do carpentry and consent to help him. "When he sees what old butterfingers made, he'll build, all right," Davey tells Goliath.

The flame picked up the rim of the paper plate, curling it backward on itself and toppling another candle. This one hit the pine needles, which instantly crackled with fire. Andrew and I stared at the screen. The show had a recurring joke about all the amenities that Goliath wanted in his doghouse, and they included wall-to-wall carpeting, an elevator, and a revolving door. Andrew and I were not yet allowed to ride the town's one elevator by our-selves, though later we practiced with my grandfather, who left us in the hotel lobby while he rode up, leaving us to call the elevator down, get on, press the right floor, and meet him in his room. We had been through the town's one revolving door at the library. Later, when my parents rebuilt the TV room, they put in wall-to-wall carpeting that was the color of faded grass.

A flame reached the curtain above the TV set, and another lit the cables behind it. The curtain, which hung down one side of a sliding glass door, had a pattern based on the Bayeux tapestry. The fire scaled it. The show played on.

"I can't build that house. Davey, your father wouldn't ask it if he didn't know you could. He wants you to learn to do things on your own. You're right on the beam. You do the actual building and I'll be your foreman. We can even figure out some things tonight."

Davey gets the lumber, and cuts it to size, but builds the house badly. All of the angles are off. He tells his pastor, impudently, "I bet you'd like it if I put a Bible verse over the door!"

The pastor scoffs, also impudent. "You're putting me on," he says. "But if you did use one, I know a verse that fits. From the book of Psalms: 'Unless the Lord builds the house, they work in vain who build it.'"

That verse, it turned out, had nothing to do with the lesson of the show, which seemed to be about doing things alone. Fire caught the woodwork around the window. Andrew and I stayed silent; our eyes didn't leave the screen. Maybe Andrew was studying colors and shapes, listening to the words he didn't understand. "Doghouse Dreamhouse" had cast a similar spell on me, though I must have known more words than Andrew did. Did I know "butterfingers"? The room filled with smoke. Our view got murkier, but we were glued, as they say, to the set. Flames were playing around the door frames, catching bits of upholstery. Christmas was so close. We should have been choking on smoke. Andrew and I liked to be in our own worlds, but sometimes we merged them. In church, we agreed on games to pass the time.

However, when, early on, we watched television together, we didn't talk. Now the television's glow brought out the haze of the burning room, and we stayed stock-still together in it.

We got out all right. When the wires got burnt all the way through, the picture on the television went to static. I called for my mother to fix it; she knew how to adjust the knobs. The fact that we hadn't seen the fire around us didn't seem shameful at the time, but my mother saw the spreading fire and yelped. First she tried to operate a fire extinguisher. She seemed sharply, irrevocably afraid; her hands shook and she quickly turned furious at herself for not knowing how to work it. Then she hustled us outside. It was a beautiful day. The three of us crossed the street, Andrew in Mom's arms, to a red house that belonged to a kind old couple named the Stimpsons.

Later Andrew and I thought we must be misremembering the whole morning, that even as kids we would, like all mammals, have perceived the smoke and scalding heat. But we can recall precisely Davey's bad doghouse with its cockeyed boards, and then we can conjure up memories of his good one, which had a removable roof. The show's haphazard parable, which even now, watching it on DVD, I can't figure out, had demanded our concentration and, swiftly, our enchantment. Maybe enchantment had defeated fear in us. And if we'd been fervidly reading books, Dr. Seuss or *Treasure Island,* then would it have been excusable for us to overlook the fire?

Though the firemen got lost, the police made it, and they put out the fire. By then the inside of the room was in ashes. My father was overjoyed to find Andrew and me eating soup at the Stimpsons'. He said that as long as we were all together, he didn't care a bit about the damage to our house; workmen could fix it while we were in London, and we could have a brand-new room. The four of us then went outside and held hands, watching our house smolder from the safety of the lawn across the road. A few days later we left for London.

The neighborhood was so goody-goody then, our bright, clean road was ideal for tricycles and then bikes. We put on plays. Children everywhere. Lemonade stands. You'd hardly believe how close our lives were to the Hansons', even though they were Lutherans and we were Episcopalians. Without thinking, I believed that God had saved us from the fire. Even as late as the seventies, it wasn't a lie that people lived like that. I thought TV got the world just about right.

HAWAII FIVE-O

Mark Leyner

When I was an undergraduate at Rensselaer Polytechnic Institute in Troy, New York, the celebrated South Korean director Jang Ki-Duk joined the faculty for a semester as a guest lecturer. He was considered at that time the king of the midget gang-bang films, which in South Korea is a perfectly respectable genre, much like Westerns here. Jang, internationally acclaimed as a virtuosic auteur, walked around campus, in the middle of the winter, five degrees below zero, in a white cowboy hat and a white jockstrap—that's it. That was his uniform. Absolute lunatic. But an unquestionable artistic genius.

Jang directed some seventy-five midget gang-bang movies before breaking out of the genre with a film called *Imwon Kyongjeji,* which doesn't include a single gang bang—a radical departure for him. *Imwon Kyongjeji* concerns a posse of super-violent Korean midget manicurists who battle a white-supremacist methamphetamine-trafficking gang in the Midwest. The film includes the infamous "salon pithing scene," in which a supremacist's spinal cord is severed with a nail file, and we're subjected to an unflinching five-minute tight shot of his hand twitching spasmodically in a dish of moisturizing lotion. (*Imwon Kyongjeji* won the coveted Palme d'Or at Cannes in 1999.) Jang's most recent film is a bukkake version of John Ford's *Fort Apache*.

At one of Jang's nine A.M. lectures at Rensselaer that semester (the topic, I recall, was "Celadon Ceramics of the Koryo Dynasty"), he mentioned, almost in passing, his notion that everything that's occurred in the world since the *Hawaii Five-O* pilot episode first aired in 1968—Watergate, Iran Contra, Robert Bork, Anita Hill, Joey Buttafuoco, Tonya Harding, O.J., Mad Cow disease, Monica—is, in fact, a hallucination of *Five-O* chief Steve McGarrett as he lies suspended facedown in the evil Wo Fat's sensory deprivation tank. I don't know how many of my bleary-eyed classmates were even aware at the time of Jang's astonishing ontological tangent—this idea that what we consensually deem to be objective is actually the traumatized delusion of a fictional television character—but I emerged from the lecture hall that morning in a state of intellectual and spiritual upheaval, and have, ever since, maintained a consuming fascination with the series and its austere, imperious star, Jack Lord.

Recently, I flew to South Korea to talk to Jang Ki-Duk about *Hawaii Five-O*. He insisted on picking me up at my hotel and driving me to a restaurant on the outskirts of Seoul he'd chosen especially for the interview.

Jang arrived accoutered in his signature white cowboy hat/white jockstrap ensemble, accessorized with a jangling assortment of biker/head shop tchotchkes on his wrist. I squeezed into the passenger seat of his black Porsche 930 next to his translator (Jang speaks virtually no English), a stylishly dressed, urbane young Korean woman given to paroxysms of girlish giggles at some of Jang's more ludicrous remarks. With Jang at the helm, we were soon out of the city proper and careening at ridiculously high speeds past chemical tanks, pressure vessels, catalytic reactors, thermal fluid heaters, and gleaming distillation columns.

"You know where this place is?" I teased.

"It's a bit off the beaten path, known only by the illuminati," Jang replied, through his translator. "The owner eschews publicity, turned down four toques in the *Michelin Guide*, didn't want the tourist trade. Very eccentric, sort of Proustian motherfucker. Asthmatic. Lined the walls of the restaurant with cork to keep out the stench . . . The tourist trade—" Jang burst into laughter, gesturing at a constellation of flaming incinerators and smoldering, gaseous exhaust stacks. "You're gonna love it, though. It's a charcuterie. Very authentic. Very Sixth Arrondissement. Foie gras, tripe, sweetbreads . . ."

He threw his head back and stomped on the throttle. "I love this fucking drive. Y'ever see *Written on the Wind*? Douglas Sirk film. Opening scene . . . Robert Stack's driving this gorgeous little yellow MG, swilling corn liquor from a bottle, tearing through his daddy's oil fields, a boulevard of drilling derricks. This is the sound track."

He slid a CD of *Written on the Wind*, the title song of which was sung by the Four Aces, into the dashboard console.

Jang maneuvered the steering wheel with the sharp, precise adjustments of a Formula One driver. And no matter how loud he turned up the music, it was drowned out by the high-pitched whine of an engine at maximum r.p.m. The road was devoid of other cars. We hurtled past more shimmering chemical tanks, flaring pylons, sulfurous efflux columns. Jang opened his window. He inhaled deeply.

"Smell that?" he asked.

"Yeah." I grimaced, my nostrils aflame with petrochemical effluvia.

"Pheromones," he said. "Ingestible information."

He inhaled again.

"I love it," he shouted, suddenly swerving the car and screeching to a stop in front of what appeared to be a polyethylene terephthalate polymer plant.

I got out of the car and was momentarily overwhelmed by the methane of cattle flatulence and sulfur wafting in from the countryside.

Even though Jang is a familiar media figure in South Korea, and a regular at this particular restaurant, a man wearing only a cowboy hat and a jockstrap still attracts a certain amount of ogling. Heads turned as we walked to our banquette. Once seated, Jang immediately got up, grasped my head in both his hands, and turned it slowly from side to side.

"This is your POV. It's your movie. Wherever you look. See? You're John Ford. You're Hou Hsiao-Hsien. And a sound track—"

He put headphones from his iPod on my head. I heard Basement Jaxx's "Kissalude."

"It's your movie, man. It's all you."

The restaurant was a traditional, quaint French charcuterie. A lustrous assortment of cuts of meat, pâtés, sausages, kidneys, and brains filled glass displays. We sipped Cokes, gazing through the window at the reactors and incinerators. Soon, without having taken our order, a waitress arrived at the table with a *croque-monsieur* for the translator, and an enormous platter for Jang and me, with foie gras, tripe, marrow, beef cheeks, medallions of blood-rare filet mignon, and Jang's favorite, a Hawaiian delicacy, SPAM musubi— four-inch rice blocks topped with SPAM and wrapped in seaweed. Jang tore into his food with unbridled ferocity and primal pleasure.

Q: Several years ago, in a lecture at Rensselaer Polytech, you said that everything that's happened in the world since the *Hawaii Five-O* pilot first aired in 1968 is actually the hallucination of

Steve McGarrett as he lies in a sensory deprivation tank. Could
you elaborate on that?

A: I think I was being a little dramatic, maybe a bit hyperbolic. But
I'd contend that, at the very least, every ensuing episode of *Hawaii
Five-O* is in fact an hallucination of Steve McGarrett. Let's not
forget that in the pilot, McGarrett allows himself to be captured by
the diabolical Chinese agent Wo Fat, who's mastered the art of
breaking prisoners by keeping them suspended for protracted periods of time in a sensory deprivation vat. McGarrett's put into this
vat and kept there far longer than anyone's ever been. It's obvious
that everything that happens in *Hawaii Five-O* is only occurring
within McGarrett's traumatized mind. And I see my own films as
an extrapolation—an endless efflorescing, if you will—of McGarrett's hallucinations. I see all of my work—the midget gang-bang
movies, *Imwon Kyongjeji, Bukkake Fort Apache*—as also existing
within the delusional mind of Steve McGarrett in Wo Fat's tank.

Q: That's so fucked up.

A: [loudly sucking marrow from a thick cylindrical bone, and
licking the juice from his fingers] I know. One can further contend that, in the vat, McGarrett—after some vast period of
time—then achieves posttraumatic satori and is transformed into
a kind of Baudelairean dandy.

Q: A Baudelairean dandy? What do you mean by that?

A: In 1860, in Paris, Baudelaire wrote an essay called "The Painter
of Modern Life," ostensibly about an artist by the name of Constantin Guys. The essay contains a brilliant disquisition on the
qualities of the "dandy"—an exemplary figure in Baudelaire. This

essay was actually written about Steve McGarrett/Jack Lord. (They're interchangeable, but more about that later.) But Baudelaire realized that he'd never be able to publish an essay about a television actor who wouldn't exist for another 108 years, so he basically did a macro "Find/Change" on his document and transposed every "Jack Lord" into "Constantin Guys."

Q: You're saying that in 1860, Charles Baudelaire wrote an essay about how Jack Lord was the exemplary "dandy"?

A: Listen to this: "The distinguishing characteristic of the dandy's beauty consists above all of an air of coldness which comes from an unshakable determination not to be moved; you might call it a latent fire which hints at itself, and which could, but chooses not to, burst into flame." Who does that sound like?

Q: Jack Lord . . . Steve McGarrett?

A: Bingo, my friend. How about this? "Dandyism borders on the spiritual and stoical. . . . It is first and foremost the burning need to create for oneself a personal originality, bounded only by the limits of the proprieties. It is a kind of cult of the self. . . . It is the joy of astonishing others, and the proud satisfaction of never oneself being astonished. . . . It is from this that the dandies obtain their haughty exclusiveness, provocative in its very coldness. . . . Dandyism is the last spark of heroism amid decadence." Ring a bell?

Q: Jack Lord.

A: And this: "Nothing is missed: his lightness of step, his stoical aplomb, the simplicity in his air of authority, his way of wearing a coat or riding a horse, his bodily attitudes, which are always relaxed but betray an inner energy, so that when your eye lights upon one of those privileged beings in whom the graceful and the formidable are so mysteriously blended, you think: a rich man perhaps, but more likely an out-of-work Hercules."

Q: Or an out-of-work Jack Lord! I see!

A: Never mind that in the fifteenth century, Zeami, the great theoretician of the Noh theater, compared the stillness of Noh to a silver vase filled with frozen snow—which is a fucking, dead-on perfect description of . . . Envelope, please . . .

Q: Jack Lord. That's amazing.

A: In the final installment of "'V' for Vashon," a three-part episode that aired in 1972, McGarrett is being framed by the patriarch of a notorious Hawaiian criminal family. He's been suspended on some trumped-up charge of having shot an unarmed man, and he temporarily retreats to a little villa somewhere out of town. It's here that McGarrett/Lord attains his apotheosis as a dandy. He wears a wide-brimmed white straw hat, pinkish scarf, white suit, and a silk shirt dappled with chrysanthemum blossoms. Even McGarrett's portrayal—his simulation—of a "dandy" is hyperaestheticized. It's a dandyfied rendition of a dandy, a laminated lamination.

Q: What does McGarrett/Lord signify?

A: Narcissim/Onanism/Solipsism/Inertia. In the guise of a dour autocrat with an imperturbably jaunty coiffure.

Q: But doesn't the term *dandy* imply a certain trivial, self-aggrandizing vanity? I don't necessarily view him that way at all.

I see McGarrett/Lord as a kind of beatified figure, as a martyr. Given those very same attributes you've alluded to—the noblesse oblige, the emphatic rectitude, the peremptory authority, the self-abnegation, the sacrifice—one might call him Saint Lord.

A: His asceticism was an ostentation, an overweening vanity . . . a voluptuously self-cannibalizing appetite.

Q: How would you describe Steve McGarrett's managerial style?

A: He ran *Five-O* like a combination Yakuza Oyabun and cult leader. His subordinates drank his bathwater.

Q: *Hawaii Five-O* ran for 278 episodes, from 1968 to 1980. If you could just speculate hypothetically . . . Had the show continued to air for, say, another 278 episodes, what would have become of McGarrett/Lord? Can you extrapolate his arc?

A: He would have ended up like that other great quintessential American Baudelairean dandy, Howard Hughes. Holed up in the Kahala Hilton Hotel on the beach at Waikiki, drapes perpetually closed, lying in bed in a black DEA sweatsuit, surrounded by piles of *TV Guide*s, injecting himself with codeine and Demerol, his arms and thighs scored with needle marks, long, filthy, unkempt hair, his fingernails like spiral jetties coiling out into the inky blackness of his abyss.

Q: Dude, what are you working on now?

A: I've always wanted to make an homage to Jean-Luc Godard's *One Plus One,* which is a movie about, well, maybe not "about"—a movie that incorporates the Rolling Stones' making of *Sympa-*

thy for the Devil. So I've begun production on a movie about four deejays who are making a remix of the *Hawaii Five-O* theme song. It's called *Hawaii Five-O vs. Frankenstein.* The deejays play themselves and improvise all their own dialogue. There's Throbbin Hood, Kid Krishna, Fluxmeister Klimax, and Cunty Orloff (the enigmatic doyenne of the febrile Amsterdam underground breakbeat scene). The only part of the movie that's scripted is when Rick Derringer—the guy who produced the Edgar Winter Group's 1972 album, *They Only Come Out at Night*—shows up at the studio one night. The kids, the deejays, go fuckin' nuts, man. Because they all dig that cut from the album, "Frankenstein." And they collaborate with Derringer on bringing that heavy-and-rolling, old-school synth vibe to the remix.

Q: What's so significant to you about the theme song?

A: In truth, the episodes themselves were merely appendices to the title sequence and the theme song. The title sequence is inexhaustibly fecund. Just that initial wave alone. It's the mutant successor to Katsushika Hokusaia's *Great Wave.* If it's true that the title sequence renders the ensuing episodes superfluous, the wave itself is so replete with meaning that it perhaps renders the remainder of the title sequence redundant. But this would be a very radical interpretation.

Q: What did you mean when you said that Steve McGarrett and Jack Lord were interchangeable?

A: One could say that the actor, Jack Lord, is actually an hallucination of Steve McGarrett as he lies in Wo Fat's sensory deprivation tank. Or that Jack Lord is an incarnation or avatar of Steve McGarrett, as, in Hindu mythology, Bhairava is an epithet of

Siva, and Varaha is the third avatara of Visnu, and Parvati and Sati, manifestations of the goddess Devi. In the most banal sense, Jack Lord was simply playing himself, and in this way, he was the absolute progenitor of today's reality television. Jack Lord is the progenitor of Andrew on *The Bachelor*, and Trista and Ryan, et cetera.

Q: Where do you think television, and specifically reality television, is going?

A: Shows that had once been considered lowbrow and stultifyingly devoid of content will soon seem like mandarin refinements compared to the fare we're about to consume. I think the recent Britney Spears interview on *20/20* where she confessed that she's been dating Robert Chambers augurs the future of TV. Everyone originally assumed that her disheveled, bruised, postcoital look was just an image makeover in pursuit of enhanced street cred, until it was revealed by Amnesty International to be the result of torture by an ABC pre-interview squad comprised of sadists from Savak, the Shah's secret police, and out-of-work Baath Party interrogation specialists. But it was a fucking ratings bonanza—35 million viewers! I think we're going to see the live, on-air torture of celebrities become immensely popular. I think we're going to see people like Zooey Deschanel, Frankie Muniz, Bijou Phillips, Jude Law, and Jennifer Aniston shackled and blindfolded and hung upside down and subjected to electric shock and having the soles of their feet beaten, and even to bellary, an Indian third-degree technique in which they take a stick and smear it with red chili powder and stick it up your anus. And I think, of course, that people will become inured to even that. And ultimately we will all affix cameras to the tops of our televisions, facing our couches, and we will sit there in front of these cameras, in gas masks and

thick forty-five-pound flak jackets, watching ourselves mastur-
bate. That's the future of reality television.

I'd prepared a parting salute to Jang—an iconic, recurring signature line of McGarrett's that I knew he'd appreciate. It seemed the
appropriate time. The afternoon had lapsed into twilight and
Jang's prescient speculations about reality TV culminating in an
infinitely recursive auto-voyeurism—an entropy of terminal narcissism—seemed to provide a satisfying sense of closure to our
conversation.

I stood up and bowed slightly.

"Book 'em, Danno," I said.

Jang's eyes widened and then rolled back in his head. He appeared to lose consciousness, and for the next several moments,
stared blankly with a fluttering movement of his lids and rapid
twitching of his fingers and mouth.

Apparently the phrase "Book 'em, Danno" had induced a
seizure during which Jang experienced an immersive, 3-D,
panoramic IMAX version of the *Hawaii Five-O* title sequence.

Each shot strobed against his fluttering eyelids: the great
foaming wave, with the words *Hawaii Five-O* in the lower right-
hand corner of the screen, and the fusillade of drums and fanfare
of horns; the montage of white buildings along the coast culminating with a nondescript high-rise; that jerking thrust into a
medium shot of Jack Lord on the balcony; and then the tight shot
of him with the words "Costarring Jack Lord" to his right; the
voluptuous girl running along the beach, suggestively touching
her hair; the moiré, iridescent water shots; the scowling visage of
some chiseled Polynesian deity; the gleaming underbellies of
planes on a runway; the frenetically undulating hips of a hula
dancer in a nightclub; a clean-cut detective peering through
an aperture of shattered glass and the kryon reading, "James

MacArthur as Dan Williams"; a burly Asian plainclothes cop on a roof speaking urgently into a walkie-talkie: "Kam Fong as Chin Ho"; the flashing light atop a police car hurtling down some street in downtown Honolulu, superimposed with "Created by Leonard Freeman."

And, as implausible as it seems, I could actually hear the *Hawaii Five-O* theme song emanating from Jang's head. It was audible. Who knows what sort of neuromonal firestorm within his brain could produce this sonic nimbus?

He regained consciousness, his forehead beaded with perspiration, his eyes glazed. He looked at me with a smirk across his face, pointing vigorously down at his jockstrapped crotch, and said something in Korean.

The young woman, giggling behind her hand, refused to interpret, until I insisted.

"Book this," she translated.

She winced with embarrassment at having reflexively indicated her own crotch.

"I mean, 'Book that,'" she said hastily, pointing at Jang's tumescent package, and then, having regained her composure, "Book that, Danno. Murder one!"

THE TWILIGHT ZONE

Alan Lightman

All of my best television memories come from the long-ago period of my childhood, in the mid-1950s to early 1960s, when I lived with my parents and three younger brothers in a redbrick two-story house in Memphis. My parents would be out for the evening. Neglecting our homework, changing into our pajamas, my brothers and I would lie like alligators on the dingy brown carpet in front of the glowing box, mesmerized. We drew straws to see who got to choose the first show. Around seven o'clock, Blanche would bring in badly burnt burgers and a great big bowl of french fries. (Blanche was the black maid who worked for our family for thirty-five years.) "Ya'll shouldn't get so close to that thing," Blanche would complain. Then she'd take a long drag on one of her Pall Malls. From time to time, especially during baseball season, Blanche watched television herself, sneaking into the sitting room when no one was home. She was a fierce fan of the Brooklyn Dodgers. She could reel off statistics. Occasionally, I would call home to confide in Blanche some inconsequential thing and hear a baseball game in progress.

Our favorite programs, much inferior to sports broadcasts in Blanche's mind, were *Superman, Amos 'n' Andy, Dragnet, Route 66, The Lone Ranger, Zorro, Alfred Hitchcock Presents,* and Rod Serling's *Twilight Zone. The Twilight Zone* frightened Blanche so much that she wouldn't venture into the sitting room if it was on. "Come in, Blanche, watch it with us," we'd plead with her. "I'm not putting one eyeball on that scary thing, and ya'll shouldn't be neither. Ya'll will be up all night asking me to sleep in your bed with you." "Blanche, we're starving. Where's our dinner?" "Ya'll will have to come to the kitchen your own selves. I'm not coming near that scary thing."

The Twilight Zone frightened us, too, and that's why we loved it. Each program began with a spine-chilling jingle, rising and falling, like the repeated clanging of two piano keys badly out of tune with each other. Even now, I don't know what demonic instrument could produce such a sound. Then, as we lay on the floor, peeking through our covered eyes, we would see an introductory scene of the show. Many horror programs and films begin with a facade of innocence and serenity, a few minutes of congenial domestic life, a happy man or woman walking about a pleasant house or fishing on a quiet pond. After the viewer is lulled into a sense of normalcy, the abnormalcy begins. But in *The Twilight Zone,* right from the start there was a sense of darkness, something on edge, a brooding quality, a foul odor from the abyss. Then Mr. Serling himself would appear on the screen, only momentarily breaking the spell, and announce that "you are about to enter the Twilight Zone." At that point, my brothers and I would begin howling in terrified delight, and Blanche would scream from the kitchen.

Rod Serling's demeanor, in his brief appearances, added a definitive gravity and weight to his imaginative creations. He would be dressed conservatively in a dark suit and tie, and he would speak in a measured, serious voice about the world of terror that lay just beyond the visible. If one turned off the sound, Serling could have been a banker talking about investments, or a university professor lecturing on British history. But, in fact, he was talking about horrifying things. He never opened his mouth very much, so that he swallowed his words almost before they escaped, yet at the same time he spoke clearly and distinctly. Somehow, this way that he talked seemed to emphasize his authority and reliability. We viewers got the impression that we were about to see a documentary, a glimpse of how the world really was. All of these features made the program even more frightening.

Forty years later, a number of episodes still remain in my mind. In one, as I remember, a man and a woman finish a meal in a Chinese restaurant, and, afterward, the dark prophecy in their fortune cookie comes true. As it turns out, this particular restaurant has a macabre power. Sometime later, the couple returns to the restaurant, and again their fortune comes to pass. Both of the prophecies are devastating but leave their victims alive. The man and the woman don't want to go back to the restaurant, they don't want to know what new and dire thing is waiting in their future, but some terrible urge draws them back, over and over again. And in one of the last scenes, we see other couples, cowering at their tables, waiting with dread for their own fortune cookies to arrive.

In another episode, the narrative begins with a woman at work in a farmhouse. She is churning butter, or stacking eggs from the henhouse. I can still see her clearly. She is a plain woman, middle-aged, dressed in rough fabric, a mole on her scowling face, and she goes about her farm business in a dour, methodical way. Throughout the episode, the woman, played by Agnes Moorehead, never speaks. In the background, beyond the farmhouse, we see fields, trees, a twilight sky, perhaps a barn. All seems familiar, but there is something not quite right about the scene. Then a fly buzzes through a window, and the woman swats at it. In fact, it is a little too large to be a fly; it has a metallic glint, and it makes a strange noise. Then another large insect buzzes in. The woman swats at it, too. She is getting annoyed. Another one, and she begins really swinging hard at the insects, getting her body into it. One of them has crashed into her, hurt her, and she screams out with pain and anger. Now she is almost demented. She is thrashing about, whirling around, making unintelligible grunts. At this point, the camera zooms in to one of the crashed fly things on the floor, and we see that it is actually a miniature spaceship. Tiny creatures wearing spacesuits stumble from their busted spaceship and radio for help. The poor woman in her desolate farmhouse has apparently been invaded by little aliens. The radio distress call crackles, and we listen in and are jolted to hear that the space creatures are radioing Earth! Then we see a face through a space helmet. It is human. In fact, the little aliens are humans. It is not that they are tiny, we suddenly realize, but rather that the woman is huge; she is a giant. She is a giant who lives on another planet, resembling Earth but not Earth. And, evidently, an expedition of spaceships from Earth has just landed in her farmhouse.

My favorite of all the episodes opens with a man lying on an operating table. Heavy bandages completely cover his face. Doctors hover over the patient, discussing his case. With careful skill, the camera shows the doctors only from their shoulders down, lending a bizarre effect to the scene. We see their gloved hands as they slowly begin to unravel the bandage around the man's head. From their comments, we infer that the physicians have just performed a massive plastic surgery on the man's face. Before the operation, he had the face of a monster, they say, a grotesquely deformed face. Such a person could never have survived in society. But they have every hope now that with the surgery, his face has been made beautiful. Layer by layer, they unwrap his face. The white bandages slowly pile up on the table. Finally, the last layer comes off. The patient has his back to the camera, so that the doctors, but not the viewer, can see him. The doctors gasp. They shriek. The operation has failed, they shout. The patient is still as monstrously ugly as before. Then the camera swings around and shows his face. Instead of the monster that we expect, he is a perfectly normal-looking, even handsome man. The camera lifts up and, for the first time, we see the faces of the doctors. They are all misshapen, grotesque, nightmarish.

The Twilight Zone, in many of its episodes and especially in these last two, managed to turn the world upside down, to twist reality so that we saw reality more clearly. That was Rod Serling's genius. His programs had irony and meaning. Every episode was true. Even as a little boy of twelve, I realized that The Twilight Zone was more than a scary TV show. The Twilight Zone suggested to me, at an unconscious level, that I was taking far too much of the world, and of life, for granted. My perspective was severely narrow. Now I appreciate the series even more. The Twilight Zone is really a place in our minds, the place of unexamined assumptions. And it can frighten us in the way that all unknown things frighten.

However, when I think back on that time of my childhood, on those nights when my brothers and I watched The Twilight Zone with the shades pulled down, the room darkened, and the flickering light of the screen throwing moving shadows about a room, I don't remember being so badly frightened. I remember more a sense of excitement. I remember Blanche's voice singing one of her church songs in the kitchen. I remember the smell of burnt burgers. I remember my brothers and me happily howling together as brothers, a few years before going our separate ways, before my brothers were engulfed in the drug-laden haze of the late 1960s, before Blanche died a suffocating death of emphysema,

PART FIVE

IN THE BEGINNING

THE WORLD in BLACK and WHITE

Sven Birkerts

The assignment I was given was to write an essay about my memories of television. The assignment I gave myself, after testing and rejecting any number of nostalgia-driven reconnaissance missions to once-beloved programs, was to write about the generic memory of black-and-white TV itself, to explore a topic that right away seemed to me packed with associations and suggestions. There was a good reason for my making the adjustment: I quickly discovered when I tried to remember specific programs I had watched—*The Donna Reed Show,* say, or *The Man From U.N.C.L.E.*—that I had almost nothing to hold on to. The contents had essentially vanished, leaving as residue only a jumble of half-remembered images, a kind of televisual bathtub ring. Whether the problem lay with my eroding brain cells or the fundamental ephemerality of those contents is a subject for another essay. What interested me at the moment of realization was the fact that while my concrete recollections were sketchy at best, the feeling of those grainy saturations of black and white, of the tonal pulse of those pixels, was vivid. I could very readily dream my way back to the impressions of that former state of things.

Association is the natural reflex of the uncensored dreaming self, and what my early televisual associations give me is nothing less than the whole buzzing, blooming (the paired adjectives belong to William James) apparition of the world as it was for me then. I mean this quite literally. Coming into the culture and my life when it did, television brought me for the first time the idea that the world was somehow an accessible totality, a coherent out-there, and that its spectral signature was black and white. By this I mean the world as implied (and referred to) by the serious newscasting presences of Chet Huntley and David Brinkley; as documented with grave voice-over on a Sunday-afternoon program called, I believe, *The Twentieth Century*; and as the implicit home base of the suited men and coiffed women who spoke from the staged environments of appliance commercials and lavishly curtained variety shows. Before—and this is almost impossible to reconstruct—I think I knew only the intensities of whatever was immediate (the yard, the street, the jumble of town) and whatever uncontextualized samples of the unknown the radio brought in.

But black-and-white TV was not just a window onto what might be called the larger out-there; it also represented the idea of the mainly decorous and serious adults who orchestrated its least activities, and who were joined together in some freemasonry of coded signals and knowing looks—who, I could almost believe, all knew one another and had secret places where they met.

That once-fashionable term: *the other*. I hesitate to bring it forward. But it fits here and helps get me closer to something of the mystery—and paradox—I'm after. It has everything to do with what I feel now as a deep chromatic split. Odd, but there it is. My parents, my teachers, the adults I knew and moved among towered over me in living color. They were all-important, but they were also, in the surprising new setting delivered by television, of merely local stature. Their bright dimensional presence did not, in terms of this authority, this covert insiderness, impress me. They were here, and now that there was TV, I knew that life was elsewhere, other; was there like some endlessly fascinating exhibit arranged inside the perimeters of the picture tube.

What I'm talking about—I grasp it now, from the remove of years—is less the phenomenon of black and white per se and more the original power of television itself. The anomalous thing is that that power revealed itself first without the illusion-enhancing richness of color, and then, once the transaction happened—once the projection was complete—black and white became its total embodiment. Illusion be damned.

Whether for economic reasons or due to some deep-seated resistance to popular gimmickry, my parents were late in buying our first television set, which means that the medium had a chance to acquire for me a considerable desirability. TV was something that other families had and congregated around (my imaginings were standard-issue Norman Rockwell on this score: intimacy warmly conjured by the glow of the picture tube, Mom and Dad arrayed protectively on either side of Buddy and Sis). Schoolyard references to various shows were, thus, inflated in my mind into scenarios rich with the subtle status of insiderdom. When Sue Dickson, Walnut Lake School's original *Gunsmoke* fan, founded her Matt Dillon fan club, I didn't even know who Matt Dillon was. I had the paranoid sense that kids all around me were all in on something.

As it happened, my old-world grandparents, who lived nearby and were much less assimilated than my parents (like them Latvian-born), actually acquired a set first, which, of course, made me far more eager than I otherwise might have been to stay with them when my parents left for one of their weekend trips to Chicago to visit old friends. But again, what I remember here has less to do with any programs I might have watched in their minuscule living room than with my extraneous associations. What I mainly recall is the ritualized seriousness they brought to the act of watching. I think of various period movies I've seen that depict entire families gathering in their living rooms after dinner to listen to variety programs on the radio. That was also the feeling of our viewing; and that was the atmospheric era of my grandparents' living room.

Watching those set-piece scenes, I study the body language. I recognize a certain intentness—the way both my grandmother and grandfather would arrange themselves in front of the set, taking care (as they did with everything that asked for movement) to ready the room by clearing a sitting space, adjusting lights, and so on. All this preliminary fussing, combined with the raptness with which they sat and hung on every word and action and facial expression of whoever they were watching (Arthur Godfrey, Huntley and Brinkley, Ed Sullivan . . .), signaled that sitting ourselves down in front of the screen was an act of devotion. I registered piety, even a kind of sanctimoniousness, and nowadays as my children fling themselves this way and that, hammering the clicker and promiscuously sampling whatever is on offer, I will sometimes think of my grandparents' hand-folded uprightness and the sheer focal intensity they brought to the ritual of "the program" and to television itself. Which was—I will emphasize it again—still something new in the world.

When we did finally get a set—Christmas Eve; I was in the third grade—the momentousness of the event was overwhelming. This was bigger than buying a new car, no question. I remember the note under the tree directing us to the box in the garage, the ceremonial hush surrounding the unwrapping, the "We've got liftoff" thrill that came when the plug was inserted, the button pushed (or pulled), and moving images of people first came alive in our house. The show was *Ozzie and Harriet,* and—it was my first postmodern moment—the Nelsons were celebrating Christmas in their own living room. I had that most gratifying sense of joining up. We had just taken a seven-league step toward being like the families up and down the street. No less important, we had punched a hole in the wall of our isolation and now the world could come streaming in.

But this is becoming more autobiographical than speculative, and what really interests me here is chasing down something that feels essential. I want to reflect on what that primary saturation of pixels has come to mean. Which is different from simply recovering what it meant back then, though the feeling of the original encounters is not irrelevant. I'm really talking about black-and-white TV as representing the arrival of a new kind of consciousness, a consciousness I would not have possessed—would not now possess—had the invention never happened. And this is intimately bound up with the particular form of its arrival.

For me, black-and-white television was not simply a precursor to color or an earlier phase on a technological continuum that has now pushed forward to embrace the high-resolution digital presentation of images. I'm talking about something grasped deep down as a difference, a difference conveyed cinematically (literally and metaphorically) by the transformation moments in *The Wizard of Oz,* where Dorothy's arrival in Oz is conveyed by a release into the enchantment of color, and in the more recent movie *Pleasantville,* where the revolt against repressive normalcy and the acceptance of the pleasure principle triggers a progressive suffusion of the black-and-white environment with rich "feeling" colors. The inferences are obvious, especially in *Pleasantville*. Color is liberation; color is sensory engagement; color represents the full available human range.

My reaction, however, is the reverse—on one deep level, anyway. No doubt retrospective nostalgia has done its work here, but for me the sensation of enchantment actually comes with the backward leap, with the transition that is the stripping away of the chromatic—the collapsing of the emblematic peacock's fan. And here I apply a different logic, proposing that, at least in an obvious figurative sense, the movement in "living color" of figures on a screen is felt to be in some basic way continuous with the surrounding world. Black and white, by contrast, is fascinatingly—and here's that word again—other. In the world, presenting the world, it nevertheless creates an environment that—because it is like, but also essentially different—also accepts associations of a different sort. At least it does for me. Because I was born when I was and grew up when I did, and because the history of communications unfolded the way it has, I was able to make what I now believe was a crucially formative link. Not only did I associate the transmissions of black-and-white television with adult authority and all of its concealed mysteries, but I further connected it to the idea of the past itself. The prior world. On the screen, behind any immediate situational complication, was the symbolic place of origins and what I suspected was the great conspiracy of the real world.

How strangely our most fundamental associations structure, and yes, falsify, the world for us. I discover that no force of common sense can fully prevail over my irrational conviction that the life of the past was lived in black and white. Even now, at some subthreshold level I always experience a slight shock of "correction" whenever I am presented with evidence to the contrary, be that a Ruisdael canvas, a shard of brightly decorated pottery, or a late-night encounter with *Ben-Hur* on the Movie Channel. Ah yes, I think, getting it yet again, the leaves on their trees were green, too. But in that split second of disbelief, I find a psychological truth that trumps mere common sense. For the world before I came, if it existed at all, was a world without color. Events unfolded in gray potentiality, as trial sketches, and people were not yet lit up with my knowing. The story of Plato's Cave—the chained dwellers all taking the shadow for the thing—is the very paradigm of this perceptual solipsism, and I tailor it to my uses here. Simply put: Consciousness and the subtle nuances of color and textured surface were not yet available in the world. They originated with me. The phantasmagoria we call life was arranged exclusively for my delectation. So I believed, and finding out otherwise, step by painful, joyous step, has been the work of my life so far.

AMOS 'N' ANDY and CIVIL RIGHTS on TV

Henry Louis Gates Jr.

In our family, the TV was located in the living room, where it functioned like a fireplace in the proverbial New England winter. I'd sit in the water in the galvanized tub in the middle of our kitchen, watching the TV in the next room while Mama did the laundry or some other chore as she watched for Daddy to come home from his second job.

Actually, I first got to know white people as "people" through their flickering images on television shows. It was the television set that brought us together at night, and the television set that brought in the world outside the Potomac Valley and Piedmont, West Virginia (population 2,565 in 1950, when I was born). We were close enough to Washington to receive its twelve channels on cable, so Piedmont was transformed from a radio culture to one with the fullest range of television, virtually overnight.

During my first-grade year, we'd watch *Superman*, *Lassie*, Jack Benny, Danny Thomas, *Robin Hood*, *I Love Lucy*, *December Bride*,

Nat King Cole (of course), *Wyatt Earp, Broken Arrow,* Phil Silvers, Red Skelton, *The $64,000 Question, Ozzie and Harriet, The Millionaire, Father Knows Best, The Lone Ranger,* Bob Cummings, *Dragnet, The People's Choice, Rin Tin Tin, Jim Bowie, Gunsmoke, My Friend Flicka, The Life of Riley, Topper, Dick Powell's Zane Grey Theater, Circus Boy,* and Loretta Young—all in prime time. My favorites were *The Life of Riley,* in part because he worked in a factory like Daddy did, and *Ozzie and Harriet,* in part because Ozzie never seemed to work at all. A year later, however, *Leave It to Beaver* swept most of the others away.

With a show like *Topper,* I felt as if I was getting a glimpse, at last, of the life that Mrs. Hudson and Mrs. Thomas and Mrs. Campbell must be leading in their big mansions on East Hampshire Street. Smoking jackets and cravats, spats and canes, elegant garden parties and martinis. People who wore suits to eat dinner! This was a world so elegantly distant from ours, it was like a voyage to another galaxy, light-years away.

Leave It to Beaver, on the other hand, was a world much closer, but just out of reach nonetheless. Beaver's street was where we wanted to live, Beaver's house was where we wanted to eat and sleep, Beaver's father's firm was where we'd have liked Daddy to work. These shows for us were about property, the property that white people could own and that we couldn't. About a level of comfort and ease at which we could only wonder. It was the world that the integrated school was going to prepare us to enter and that, for Mama, would be the prize.

Of course, the other side of this particular exposure to the white man's world was that we weren't going to learn how to be colored by watching television. Seeing somebody colored on TV was an event.

"Colored, colored, on Channel Two," you'd hear someone shout. Somebody else would run to the phone while yet another hit the front porch, telling all the neighbors where to see it. And *everybody* loved *Amos 'n' Andy*—I don't care what people say today. For the colored people, the day they took *Amos 'n' Andy* off the air was one of the saddest days in Piedmont, about as sad as the day of the last mill pic-a-nic.

What was special to us about *Amos 'n' Andy* was that their world was *all* colored, just like ours. Of course, *they* had their colored judges and lawyers and doctors and nurses, which we could only dream about—and we *did* dream about those things. Kingfish ate his soft-boiled eggs delicately, out of an egg cup. He even owned an acre of land in Westchester County, which he sold to Andy, using the facade of a movie set to fake a mansion. As far as we were concerned, the foibles of Kingfish and Calhoun the lawyer were the foibles of individuals who happened to be funny. Nobody was likely to confuse them with the colored people we knew, no more than we'd confuse ourselves with the entertainers and athletes we saw on TV or in *Ebony* or *Jet,* the magazines we devoured to keep up with what was happening with the race. And people took special relish in Kingfish's malapropisms. "I denies the allegation, Your Honor, and I resents the alligator."

In one of my favorite episodes of *Amos 'n' Andy,* "Kingfish Becomes a Press Agent," Andy Brown is hired to advertise a brand of coffee and is required to dress up as a turbaned Oriental potentate. Kingfish gets the bright idea that if he dresses up as a potentate's servant, the two of them can enjoy a vacation at a luxury hotel for free. So attired, the two promenade around the lobby, running up an enormous tab and generously dispensing "rubies" and "diamonds" as tips. The plan goes awry when people try to redeem the gems and discover them to be colored glass. It was widely suspected that this episode was what prompted two Negroes in Baltimore to dress like African princes and demand service in a segregated four-star restaurant. Once it was clear to the management that these were not American Negroes, the two were treated royally. When the two left the restaurant, they took off their African headdresses and robes and enjoyed a hearty laugh at the restaurant's expense. "They weren't like our Negroes," the maître d' told the press in explaining why he had agreed to seat the two "African princes."

The simple truth is that the civil rights era came late to Piedmont, but it came early to our television set. We could watch what was going on Elsewhere on television, but the marches and sit-ins were as remote to us as, in another way, was the aspect of *Amos 'n' Andy's* all-colored world that was populated with black lawyers, black judges, black nurses, black doctors.

So civil rights took us all by surprise, and every night we'd wait until the news to see what "Dr. King and dem" were doing.

In 1957, when I was in second grade, black children integrated Central High School in Little Rock, Arkansas. And we watched it on TV. All of us watched it. I don't mean Mama and Daddy and my brother, Rocky. I mean *all* the colored people in America watched it, together, with one set of eyes. We'd watch it in the morning, on the *Today* show on NBC, before we'd go to school; we'd watch it in the evening on the news, with Edward R. Murrow on CBS; we'd watch the special bulletins at night, interrupting our TV shows.

The children were all well scrubbed and greased down, as we'd say. The boys' hair short and closely cropped, parted, and oiled; the girls' "done" in a "permanent" and straightened, with turned-up bangs and curls. Starched shirts, white, and creased pants, shoes shining like a buck private's spit-shine. Those Negroes were *clean*. The fact was, those children trying to get the right to enter that school in Little Rock looked like black versions of models out of *Jack and Jill* magazine, to which my mama had subscribed for me so that I could see what children outside the Valley were up to. "They handpicked those children," Daddy would say. "No dummies, no nappy hair, heads not too kinky, lips not too thick, no disses and dats." At seven, I was dismayed by his cynicism. It bothered me somehow that those children would have been chosen, rather than just having shown up or volunteered or been nearby in the neighborhood.

Daddy was jaundiced about the civil rights movement, and especially about the Rev. Dr. Martin Luther King Jr. He'd say all of his names, to drag out his scorn. By the mid-sixties, we'd argue about King from sunup to sundown. Sometimes he'd just mention King to get a rise from me, to make a sagging evening more interesting, to see if I had *learned* anything real yet, to see how long I could think up counterarguments before getting so mad that my face would turn purple. I think he just liked the color purple on my face, liked producing it there.

But Daddy was not of two minds about those children in Little Rock. They would get off their school bus surrounded by soldiers from the National Guard and by a field of state police. They would stop at the steps of the bus and seem to take a very deep breath. Then the phalanx would start to move slowly along the gully of sidewalk and rednecks that connected the steps of the school bus with the white wooden double doors of the school. All kinds of crackers would be lining that gully. Cheerleaders from the all-white school that was desperately trying to stay that way were dressed in those funny little pleated skirts, with a big red *C* for "Central" on their chests, and they'd wave their pom-poms and start to cheer, "Two, four, six, eight—We don't want to integrate!" And all those crackers and all those rednecks would join in that chant as if their lives depended on it. Deafening, it was; even on our twelve-inch TV, a three-inch speaker buried along the back of its left side.

We watched people getting hosed and cracked over their

heads, people being spat upon and arrested, rednecks siccing fierce dogs on women and children, our people responding by singing and marching and staying strong. Eyes on the prize. Eyes on the prize. George Wallace at the gate of the University of Alabama, blocking Autherine Lucy's way. Charlayne Hunter at the University of Georgia. President Kennedy interrupting our scheduled program with a special address, saying that James Meredith will *definitely* enter the University of Mississippi; and saying it like he meant it (unlike Ike), saying it like the big kids said "It's our turn to play" on the basketball court and walking all through us as if we weren't there.

Whatever tumult our small screen revealed, though, the dawn of the civil rights era could be no more than a spectator sport in Piedmont. It was like watching the Olympics or the World Series when somebody colored was on. Or like watching a war being fought overseas. And all things considered, white and colored Piedmont got along pretty well in those years, the fifties and early sixties. At least as long as colored people didn't try to sit down in the Cut-Rate or at the Rendezvous Bar, or eat pizza at Eddie's, or buy property, or move into the white neighborhoods, or dance with, date, or dilate upon white people. Not to mention try to get a job in the craft unions at the paper mill. Or have a drink at the white VFW, or join the white American Legion, or get loans at the bank, or just generally get out of line. Other than that, colored and white got on pretty well.

GRACIE and ME

Lloyd Schwartz

It's just possible that my love of language, my *interest* in language—puns, spoonerisms, malapropisms, turns of phrase, and the sounds of a voice *saying* them (elements that have become essential ingredients of my poems)—began with Gracie Allen, whose quintessential characteristic was the capacity to "deconstruct" phrases. *The George Burns and Gracie Allen Show* was one of my favorite shows on the radio, and then, from 1950 to 1958, on television. I think it's the funniest and most inventive situation comedy ever broadcast, without which at least one of the best later TV sitcoms—*Seinfeld*—would be inconceivable. Here (as also in another show that moved to television from radio, *The Jack Benny Show*) were well-known figures who played themselves, using their own names, and creating consistent "characters" that may or may not have reflected their real personalities, coexisting with other regular characters, both real (like their announcer, Harry Von Zell, who played an announcer named Harry Von Zell) and fictional (Blanche and Harry Morton, the inevitable next-door neighbors, played by Bea Benaderet and Hal

March, who was followed by John Brown, a victim of the black-list, Fred Clark, and finally Larry Keating). The situations often seemed to be suggested by things that could have actually happened, just as several seasons of *Seinfeld* episodes opened with Jerry Seinfeld (or "Jerry Seinfeld") doing his nightclub act, riffing on the subject that the remaining half hour of plot fed into—underlining the idea that Real Life is the source of Art.

But no sitcom ever played with the medium as thoroughly as *Burns and Allen*. At the beginning of each episode, a curtain opened on the set, clearly an artifice—a front yard, rooms in a house, a counter in a shop. George Burns leaned against a proscenium to deliver a monologue (a soliloquy?) that commented on the action of the plot. In later episodes, he actually watched a television set in his study that allowed him to spy on the other characters in the show, giving him privileged information and the power to alter the action (how I wished, as a child, that I had the equipment to do that). And the show always closed with George and Gracie, at their front door, doing one of their vaudeville routines. (Take that, Jerry Seinfeld! Take that, Marshall McLuhan!)

Suddenly, in the late 1980s, this inspired enterprise was no longer just a distant memory. A local UHF station in Boston (Channel 38) started showing the original *Burns and Allen* TV series. Now that I was grown up, I seemed to be watching the history of television and discovering that something like Shakespearean comedy (and there are numerous Shakespearean elements in *B&A*) not only preceded Neil Simon's "realism" but was also better—smarter, richer, funnier. And that the show's writers (who included Paul Henning, Sid Dorfman, Harvey Helm, and William Bums) were much more interested—consciously interested—in language. "Almost everything I know today I learned by listening to myself when I was talking about things I didn't understand," Gracie says. The puns and other plays on words could be outrageous. One breathtaking exchange (this was, after all, the 1950s) has Gracie discovering that a neighbor has been offered the choice between having her face lifted "or the Bahamas." Gracie thinks her friend should opt for the face-lift and worry about "her Bahamas" later. Gracie's lineage stems from Shakespeare's Bottom and Dogberry and Goldsmith's Mrs. Malaprop.

I came late to taking popular culture seriously. In college, intellectual issues were reserved for the books and poems I was assigned in class. I still loved radio and TV and the movies and comic books (the first of my numerous "collections") only for themselves, as in my childhood, not particularly as something to think about, but with a passion. I remember an incident when I was four—the year before I started school. My parents took me to visit my aunt and uncle in Cleveland. It was my first train trip. And it was Halloween. This would be my first experience of trick-or-treating, with my cousins. I had a wonderful time. But as I was unloading my treasure back at my aunt and uncle's house, someone must have mentioned that the day was a Tuesday, and I suddenly realized I had missed one of my favorite radio shows, *Baby Snooks* (with a very grown-up Fanny Brice doing the voice of the mischievous little girl). I was inconsolable. What was trick-or-treating compared to a beloved radio show?

The more intellectual credentials I accumulated, the more I came to value what wasn't part of the academic curriculum. In graduate school, I discovered that some of my closest friends also loved the movies and radio programs I loved as a child. And that it was all right to think about them and why they were seminal in developing our adult sensibilities.

Watching the rebroadcasts of *Burns and Allen*, I was hooked all over again. Maybe more than ever. Jokes based on both language and character—how rare these have been on television. Not to mention Gracie Allen herself—her dazzling timing, her impeccable delivery. And of course the real joke was that her "misuse" of language was always a revelation, a way of reaching some deeper truth, however lighthearted and unwitting, leaving us to wonder if the sudden profundity was truly accidental or unintentional: "When I misunderstand what you say, I always know what you're talking about." Isn't this more like a philosophy than just the quirks of a comic characterization? This word *play* is subtler and trickier than, say, *I Love Lucy*'s hilarious "Vitameatavegamin" routine. Lucille Ball, a master of the TV image, also had a radio show, but she had less concern for words themselves than for facial expressions and other physical—*visual*—comedy. It was television, not radio, that made her a star.

There are other exhilarating aspects of "Gracie Allen." One is how dangerous she was—how really destructive to property and reputation her "misunderstandings" could be. In the early films, the danger was even greater. Gracie's character was certainly tamed for radio and TV. But even on television, Gracie's misapprehensions proved costly for those around her. You could never predict what havoc she would wreak.

Another element *Seinfeld* inherited from George and Gracie, and one of their most appealing qualities, was how they were never puffed up about their celebrity. They're invited to fancy Hollywood parties. They have famous friends. They have a TV show. But they're neither surprised nor offended when they're not recognized. They don't expect the world to grovel at their feet. Lucy yearns for fame; Gracie is indifferent to hers.

Her utter lack of self-importance is part of her charm. Her genuine charm. It's one of the givens of the show that she's attractive. Lovable. And who could disagree? It's too bad that the half-hour sitcom format offered Gracie so few occasions to sing or dance. To experience that side of her, you have to turn to her movies: *Damsel in Distress*, a Fred Astaire musical with a Gershwin score (the sequence in the amusement park with Burns and Allen and Astaire won director George Stevens an Oscar), or *College Swing*, in which she sings a love song to a bewitched Edward Everett Horton ("You're a Natural," accompanied by an orchestra on his car radio), then goes into an irresistible, lighter-than-air clog dance. In *Two Girls and a Sailor* she plays a hilarious, pre–John Cage piano concerto for one finger, with the great Russian conductor Albert Coates leading the orchestra.

But at the heart of what makes Gracie so appealing is the way that because her naïveté seems so genuine, and so thorough, her feelings never appear false—especially her feelings for George. Behind everything she says or does is a fundamental combination of logic and sincerity. How could anything be other than she thinks it is?

Captivated, I started to tape the shows, and replay them, not with any ulterior motive, just for the sheer pleasure of rewatching the episodes. But one—the most extraordinary—was a turning point. It was the episode in which Gracie opens a phony telegram intended for George. It's Harry Von Zell's ploy to get George out of a seasick weekend on his sponsor's yacht—forcing him to stay home because Gracie is suffering a terminal illness. Gracie's immediate response—both logical and loving—is to make sure George will get a good new wife. I was surprisingly moved through my laughter by this remarkable act of generosity, of love. And by my knowledge that the real Gracie Allen had really died (she retired from show business in 1958 and died in 1964). That was the seed—and I wasn't conscious of it at first— that wanted to grow into a poem, that brain-itch, that worrisome bit of nagging that's the starting point for all my poems. I re-watched this episode more than any of the others. It was the one I mentioned to my friends. I didn't think of it as necessarily "poetic" or as a subject for poetry, but I couldn't let go of it, and the idea to make a poem of it began to take over. Within a few weeks, I was obsessed.

I started to read George Burns's memoirs and was struck by how devoted to Gracie he remained, long after her death. Theirs was a real love story. I also knew that I wanted to incorporate more of their "voices"—to expand their stories beyond this one episode. And I wanted to capture in my poem the unsettling interplay of fiction (the TV plots) and real life (their actual biography), just as these intersected on the show itself.

The poem, "Goodnight, Gracie," became a sequence of three unrhymed sonnets (the appropriate form for a love poem). The situations and quotations in it are from actual episodes in the series. The first sonnet is based on the thirty-ninth episode, first aired on August 10, 1954 (the party the Burnses are returning from was given by Barbara Stanwyck); the second is based on a much later episode, the 181st, "The English Playwright," telecast on March 19, 1956, with their son Ronnie, who was never a child character earlier in the series, already a college student; the new-wife episode is #131, and was first telecast on April 4, 1955. Every show ended with George wrapping up the closing routine by saying, "Say good night, Gracie," and Gracie, addressing the audience in her most gracious voice, saying "Good night." Contrary to popular belief, she never stooped to the easy joke of simply repeating "Good night, Gracie." (The original air dates, episode numbers, and titles I learned years later from a book I found in the library called *Say Good Night, Gracie! The Story of George Burns & Gracie Allen*, by Cheryl Blythe and Susan Sackett.) The prose passage is from one of George's memoirs, *Gracie: A Love Story*.

"Goodnight, Gracie" was a crucial poem for me, and became the title poem of my next book. I hoped that as the title character, Gracie would be taken as a kind of muse of absurd situations, nonlinear logic, and the unexpected possibilities of language—maybe a truer muse for my poetry than any classical one. It was my most conscious declaration that comedy in poetry could be as deep a source of poignancy as more overtly painful subjects, that (as in Shakespeare) the shadow of mortality is as present in comedy as in tragedy. I think of the poem as both a love poem, my tribute to Gracie Allen and her subversive comic spirit, and an elegy—for Gracie herself, of course, and for the most imaginative comedy series in the history of commercial television.

ᗡ ᗡ ᗡ

GOODNIGHT, GRACIE
For Gracie Allen, 1906–1964

"Almost everything I know today I learned by listening to myself when I was talking about things I didn't understand."

"Mrs. Burns, I love that zany character of yours."
"So do I, or else I wouldn't have married him."

"You mean you understand it?"
"Well, of course! When I misunderstand what you say, I always know what you're talking about."

Home very late from a Hollywood party, George and Gracie can hear their phone ringing, but can't find the key to get in. George is vexed, and tired, but Gracie is dying to wake Blanche Morton next door and gossip about dancing with

Gary Cooper: "His belt buckle ruined my gardenia!" Soon the Mortons are locked out ("Gracie, did you close the door?" "No, but I will!"); the locksmith's tools locked in (will his jealous new wife ever believe this?); and the phone never stops. . . . Day breaks, and George breaks in through a window. "I've got a wonderful idea," he announces. "From now on, we'll leave a door-key under the mat." "But I put one there *months* ago," Gracie argues, "and we couldn't get in last night." The telephone again: Who's been trying to get through? "Gracie, who was on the phone?" "I was."

ㅁ ㅁ ㅁ

"It's not a matter of whether I'm right or wrong—it's a matter of principle."

"Men are so deceitful. They look you right in the eye while they're doing things behind your back."

"Don't rush me. It isn't easy to make up the truth."

Ronnie's dying for a part in a new play whose famous author is fascinated by Gracie, but the only role still open is intended for a middle-aged actress, sole support of her widowed mother. . . . "I'm a widow too," Gracie fibs, "and Ronnie supports me!" Smitten, the playwright invites her to dine in his room. "My husband died in a shipwreck," she embroiders, "on our honeymoon." "Lucky you survived!" "Oh, I wasn't there." In breezes Ronnie, and asks for "Dad." Gracie (thinking fast): "He can never forget his father." Playwright (bewildered): "But he never knew him." Gracie (triumphant): "If he knew him, he'd forget him!" Enter "the Widow Morton" with Ronnie's long-lost father, to unravel Gracie's tangled web. . . . Blushing, the playwright offers Ronnie a part; Ronnie's in heaven; Gracie's forgiven; the playwright, like George himself, resigned to applaud her irresistible assassinations.

⌷ ⌷ ⌷

"I may not be here long."
"Where are you going?"
"Oh don't I wish I knew!"

"I didn't think people felt this wonderful when they were going. But, then again, this is the first time I've gone."

"If you ask me a question and I don't answer, don't be nervous. Just take your hats off."

. . . How casually we treated Gracie's illness. Those pills made me feel very secure. I figured we could go on this way year after year—it never entered my mind that anything would change it. Then one evening Gracie had another one of her attacks. I gave her the pill, we held on to each other—but this time it didn't work. When the pain continued, I called Dr. Kennamer, and they rushed Gracie to the hospital. . . . Two hours later Gracie was gone.

"He's crazy about dancing. His new wife has got to be a very good dancer." Gracie thinks she's dying, having opened by mistake Harry Von Zell's telegram meant to save George from a weekend seasick on his sponsor's yacht: EXAMINED YOUR WIFE CONDITION SERIOUS URGE YOU NOT TO LEAVE HER. . . . "I'm a very sick woman, but my health is so good, I didn't even know it!" She's had three agencies send over their most attractive candidates to replace "the late Mrs. Burns": "Sounds like it won't be easy to fill *her* shoes." "What size do you wear?" "How old was she when she passed on?" "Well, I'd rather not say—she hasn't passed on far enough for that." George, however, has already chosen his next wife, who—relieved, reprieved—would rather George hadn't explained: "It's such a letdown. After this, how can I be gay about an ordinary thing like living?"

ABOUT THE CONTRIBUTORS

RICHARD BAUSCH is the author of nine novels, including *In the Night Season* and *Hello to the Cannibals*. His story collections include *Selected Stories, Someone to Watch Over Me*, and *The Stories of Richard Bausch*. His short fiction has appeared in *The Atlantic Monthly, Esquire, The New Yorker, GQ, Playboy, Harper's*, and other magazines and has been widely anthologized. A member of the Fellowship of Southern Writers, he is Heritage Professor of Writing at George Mason Univeristy and lives in rural Virginia with his wife, Karen.

APRIL BERNARD's books of poetry are *Blackbird Bye Bye, Psalms*, and *Swan Electric*. She is also the author of a novel, *Pirate Jenny*, and numerous essays and book reviews. She teaches at Bennington College.

SVEN BIRKERTS is the author of five books of essays, including *The Gutenberg Elegies: The Fate of Reading in an Electronic Age* and a memoir, *My Sky Blue Trades*. A member of the core faculty of the Bennington Writing Seminars, he also teaches at Mt. Holyoke College and edits the literary journal *Agni*, based at Boston University.

LAN SAMANTHA CHANG is the author of *Hunger: A Novella and Stories* and a novel forthcoming in 2004. Her fiction has been published in *Ploughshares, The Atlantic Monthly,* and *The Best American Short Stories.* She is the recipient of fellowships from the Radcliffe Institute, Princeton University, and the National Endowment for the Arts.

SUSAN CHEEVER's eleventh book, a biography of Bill Wilson, a co-founder of Alcoholics Anonymous, will be published next year. She teaches at the Bennington Writing Seminars, writes a column for *Newsday,* and lives in New York City, where she watches television every day.

NORA EPHRON is an essayist, screenwriter, and film director. Her many pictures include *Heartburn* and *When Harry Met Sally . . .*

HENRY LOUIS GATES JR. is W. E. B. DuBois Professor of Humanities and Chair of the Department of Afro-American Studies at Harvard. He writes regularly for *The New Yorker* and other publications. His books include *Figures in Black, The Signifying Monkey,* and *Colored People.*

MICHAEL GORRA was born in New London, Connecticut, and now lives with his wife and daughter in Northampton, Massachusetts, where he teaches courses in the history of the novel at Smith College. He reviews new fiction regularly for both British and American newspapers, and is the author of *The English Novel at Mid-Century, After Empire: Scott, Naipaul, Rushdie,* and *The Bells in Their Silence: Travels Through Germany.*

BARRY HANNAH is the author of twelve books of fiction, including *Airships, Ray, The Tennis Handsome, High Lonesome,* and *Yonder Stands Your Orphan.* He's twice been nominated for the National Book Award and recently received the PEN/Malamud Award for short fiction. He lives in Oxford, Mississippi, with his wife, Susan, and their six dogs.

VIRGINIA HEFFERNAN is the television critic for *Slate* and the *New York Times.*

NICK HORNBY is the author of three novels and two nonfiction books, most recently *Songbook.* He is also the editor of an anthology of short stories, *Speaking with the Angel*. He's gone off *24* but he's a big fan of *Curb Your Enthusiasm*. He lives, works, and watches telly in North London.

MARK LEYNER is the author of five books, *I Smell Esther Williams; My Cousin, My Gastroenterologist; Tooth Imprints on a Corn Dog; The Tetherballs of Bougainville*; and *Et Tu, Babe*, from which he has cowritten a screenplay. He's recently written several episodes of ABC's *Wonderland* and a comedy pilot for the FX network. His fiction and nonfiction have appeared in *The New Yorker, Time, GQ*, the *New York Times*, and *Travel + Leisure*. He's working on a new book for Little, Brown.

ALAN LIGHTMAN is a physicist, essayist, novelist, and educator. He has been on the faculties of Harvard and MIT. His essays and reviews have appeared in *The Atlantic Monthly, Harper's, The New Yorker, The New York Review of Books*, and other magazines. He is the author of a dozen books, including the international bestseller *Einstein's Dreams* and *The Diagnosis*, which was a finalist for the 2000 National Book Award in fiction. His latest novel is *Reunion*.

STEPHEN MCCAULEY is the author of four novels, including *The Object of My Affection* and *True Enough*. He has taught writing and literature at Brandeis University, Wellesley College, and other schools. In 1998 he was named a Chevalier in the Order of Arts and Letters by the French Ministry of Culture.

JILL MCCORKLE, a native of North Carolina, is the author of five novels and three short-story collections, most recently *Creatures of Habit*. She teaches in the MFA Program in Writing at Bennington College and lives near Boston with her husband and two children.

ELIZABETH MCCRACKEN is the author of three books: *Here's Your Hat, What's Your Hurry?, The Giant's House*, and *Niagara Falls All Over Again*. She learned to read watching *Sesame Street* on a black-and-white TV, and was amazed to discover, some years later, what color Big Bird actually was.

JAMES ALAN MCPHERSON's books include *Hue and Cry*, *Railroad*, *Elbow Room*, for which he won the Pulitzer Prize in fiction, *The View from Exile*, and many others. His stories have appeared widely and have been selected for *The O'Henry Prize Stories*, *The Best American Short Stories*, and *The Best American Short Stories of the Century*. He has won fellowships and awards from the Guggenheim Foundation, the Lannan Foundation, and the MacArthur Foundation. A contributing editor at *The Atlantic Monthly*, he is a professor of English at the University of Iowa.

SUSAN PERABO is Writer in Residence and an associate professor of English at Dickinson College in Carlisle, Pennsylvania. She is also on the MFA faculty at Queens University in Charlotte, North Carolina. She is the author of a novel, *The Broken Places*, and a collection of short stories, *Who I Was Supposed to Be*.

JAYNE ANNE PHILLIPS is the author of two widely anthologized collections of stories, *Fast Lanes* and *Black Tickets*, and three novels, *Motherkind*, which was nominated for the Orange Prize, *Shelter*, and *Machine Dreams*. Her works have been published in nine languages. She is the recipient of a Guggenheim fellowship, two National Endowment for the Arts fellowships, a Bunting fellowship, and a National Book Critics Circle Award nomination. She was awarded both the Sue Kaufman Prize and an Academy Award in Literature by the American Academy and Institute of Arts and Letters. She is currently Writer in Residence at Brandeis University.

PHYLLIS ROSE is professor of English at Wesleyan University and the author of *Parallel Lives* and other works of biography, including *Woman of Letters: The Life of Virginia Woolf*, *Jazz Cleopatra: Josephine Baker in Her Time*, and a memoir, *The Year of Reading Proust*. Her son, Ted Rose, is also a writer. She started watching TV in 1948. Her favorite shows, over that time, have included *The Milton Berle Show*, *The $64,000 Question*, *What's My Line?*, *You Bet Your Life*, *Sergeant Bilko*, *The Ed Sullivan Show*, *The Avengers*, *The Man from U.N.C.L.E.*, *Hart to Hart*, *Magnum, P.I.*, *The Rockford Files*, *Dynasty*, *Hill Street*

Blues, L.A. Law, Northern Exposure, Cagney & Lacey, N.Y.P.D. Blue, Law & Order, La Femme Nikita, The Sopranos, Six Feet Under, and *The Amazing Race,* as well as *Survivor.* Her Yorkie is named Vinnie Terranova for the undercover DEA agent on *Wiseguy.*

DOUGLAS RUSHKOFF is the author of nine books, which have been translated into more than twenty languages, and include *Media Virus, Corercion, Ecstasy Club,* and, most recently, *Nothing Sacred: The Truth About Judaism.* His commentaries air on NPR's *All Things Considered* and CBS's *Sunday Morning,* and his columns appear in periodicals including the *New York Times, Time,* and *Rolling Stone.* He is a professor of communications at NYU, and lectures about media, art, society, and religion. His television work includes the documentary *The Merchants of Cool,* for PBS's *Frontline.*

LLOYD SCHWARTZ is Frederick S. Troy Professor of English at the University of Massachusetts Boston, classical music editor of *The Boston Phoenix,* and a regular commentator for NPR's *Fresh Air* and the website TomPaine.com. His most recent book of poems is *Cairo Traffic,* and he is currently co-editing the collected works of Elizabeth Bishop for the Library of America. His poems, articles, and reviews have appeared in *The New Yorker, The Atlantic Monthly, Vanity Fair, The New Republic, The Paris Review,* and *The Best American Poetry.* In 1994 he was awarded the Pulitzer Prize for criticism.

DAVID SHIELDS's forthcoming book is *Body Politic: The Great American Sports Machine.* His other books include *Black Planet: Facing Race During an NBA Season,* a finalist for the National Book Critics' Circle Award, and *Remote: Reflections on Life in the Shadow of Celebrity,* which received the PEN/Revson Foundation fellowship. His essays and stories have appeared in the *New York Times Magazine, Harper's, Yale Review, The Village Voice, McSweeney's, Slate,* and *Salon.*

791.4575 Prime times.
PRI

$23.00